CANADIA

Perspectives on Canadian Culture

CANADIAN FILM

David Clandfield

Toronto   OXFORD UNIVERSITY PRESS   1987

TO MY MOTHER

Canadian Cataloguing in Publication Data
Clandfield, David
Canadian film

(Perspectives on Canadian culture)
Bibliography: p.
Includes index.
ISBN 0-19-540581-1

1. Moving-pictures—Canada—History and criticism.
2. Moving-picture industry—Canada—History.
I. Title.   II. Series.

PN1993.5.C58   1987   791.43′0971   C87-094928-4

CONTENTS

PREFACE

In the early 1970s I was invited to join a team of writers working on a history of film in Canada. We had a publisher and soon divided the labour and began work on outlines, grant applications, and sample chapters. There was then no history of Canadian film in English and we hoped to make a contribution to the understanding of Canadian film culture and perhaps even help to stimulate the Canadian film industry. Gradually we learned of other projects: books by John Hofsess, Robert Fulford, Robert Fothergill, and Martin Knelman were all rumoured to be in the offing. Our group began to disperse and Bruce Elder and I eventually published chapters from the book as articles elsewhere. In the meantime, Hofsess's book turned out to be a journalistic report on interviews with ten film-makers, Fulford's and Knelman's were anthologies of their film reviews (though Knelman provided some historical background and bridging material), and Fothergill's faded away (a portion appeared in *Cinema Canada*). There was still no comprehensive history of Canadian film in English. When my colleague Barrie Hayne kindly suggested that I might be interested in writing a survey of Canadian Film for Oxford University Press, the opportunity to revive the project was irresistible.

The format of the 'Perspectives on Canadian Culture' has influenced the shape of this survey. In order to make the range of film-making in Canada intelligible to a broad readership, I have adopted the taxonomy usually favoured by traditional film-historians, as well as film-making and granting agencies: documentary film, fictional film, animated film, and experimental film. Within those categories, the works are grouped by director and the directors by certain broad preoccupations they shared, their origins, or their institutional affiliations. (The abbreviation **CFA** has been used throughout to signify Canadian Film Awards, which over the years have been variously referred to as Etrogs and Genies.) In the interests of space, filmmakers usually receive one detailed mention even when this means including documentaries in the fictional chapter, or otherwise tainting the categorial purity of the chapter divisions. The Canadian film tradition, with its taste for hybrid forms—docudrama, experimental narrative, combined animation and live-action, and so on—renders the boundaries of such divisions porous and arbitrary at the best of times.

In the process of compiling this work, I have accumulated many debts along the way. Ben Shek and Bruce Elder stimulated my initial research and have done much to encourage me since. I am grateful to the Department of French at the University of Toronto for research funding assistance and to Laura Uyenaka for her bibliographic work. For the wealth of detailed research required by a survey such as this, all historians of Canadian film owe much to the pioneers in the field: Peter Morris, Peter Harcourt, Piers Handling, Gilles Marsolais, Pierre Véronneau, Seth Feldman, Bruce Elder, Michael Dorland, and countless others. I have enjoyed the editorial assistance of William Toye and Patricia Sillers, who have been thorough, gracious, and supportive even when I must have strained their patience to superhuman levels. Finally, I thank my family: Sandra as my first reader and voice of encouragement, and Lindsay and William for their acceptance of the compromises writing brings to family life.

FROM ORIGINS TO GRIERSON: 1896–1939

THE COMING OF FILM TO CANADA

The first projection of motion pictures in Canada was a demonstration of the French Cinématographe on 27 June 1896 at 78 rue Saint-Laurent in Montreal. Ecstatically reviewed in *La Presse*, it did a roaring business for two months. A combined camera/projector patented in France by the Lumière brothers of Lyons, the Cinématographe had been used for the world's first public projection of moving pictures in Paris on 28 December 1895. The report in *La Presse* suggests that the Montreal show included several of the minute-long films from the historic Paris showing: the arrival of a train, a small boat going out to sea, the Lumières playing cards, the demolition of a wall, and so on. Before Germain Lacasse documented this screening in 1984, it had been thought that the Holland brothers of Ottawa had organized the first picture shows in that city with a demonstration of Edison's Vitascope on 21 July 1896.

This new phenomenon was soon absorbed into the popular culture of the time and by 1900 had spread throughout Canada, first in temporary storefronts and music-halls in cities and then in travelling road shows from coast to coast. By 1908 permanent film theatres were open for every taste and pocket from Léo-Ernest Ouimet's luxurious 1000-seat Ouimetoscope in Montreal to John Griffin's cut-price Theatorium in Toronto, the first of the Canadian Nickelodeons. In Brantford the Allen brothers, Jules and Jay, had opened their Theatorium, the first of a country-wide chain of movie theatres; there were 53 in 1923 when the chain was swallowed up by the American-based Famous Players.

The films seen by the first generation of Canadian moviegoers were one-minute moving snapshots, mute testimony to the realism of the photographic image and the illusion of continuous movement. Their subjects were everyday local scenes whose reality could not be doubted by the spectator. There were also mini-scenes of music-hall turns and circus acts that integrated the picture show into its immediate cultural context. Soon scenes were strung together to tell a story in a series of tableaux that drew inspiration from the emerging comic strip and waxworks museums where tableau representation was a standard form of display.

The travelling picture shows seem to have survived longer in francophone Quebec, where they were adapted to serve the goal of cultural survival through preservation of language, rural values, and traditional Catholic faith. From 1905, Wilfrid Picard, churchman Benjamin Paradis, and others toured with picture shows of a broadly religious flavour. The most ambitious such project in Quebec was the Historiographe of the French Viscount Henry de Grand'saignes d'Hauterives, who from 1897 toured Quebec for eleven years with Biblical tableau films, Georges Méliès' trick-films, and other standard fare from France.

FIRST FILMS MADE IN CANADA

By 1900 mini-films were including moving snapshots of natural sights. The first Canadian 'scenics' were dominated by Niagara Falls, but film-makers soon offered scenes of Canada from coast to coast, often taken from a moving CPR train. To these were added news events such as Royal Visits and the Klondike Gold Rush. Control of the industry rested with the foreign companies that had developed the technology, and film-makers suffered the same degree of anonymity as calendar photographers. Any sense of film as an art-form still lay far in the future.

Alongside the first Canadian film theatre entrepreneurs the major forces in the Canadian film industry were sponsoring companies like Massey-Harris of Toronto, which commissioned Edison to film their farm machinery, or the Canadian Pacific Railway, which frequently used film to promote land settlement in Western Canada (with the prudent stipulation that snow scenes were to be avoided). Early CPR productions included 'Living Canada' (1903–4), a series of thirty-five 'scenics' from coast to coast, and in 1910 another series of thirteen films using dramatic and comic elements. In many of the latter honest immigrant men were shown triumphing over the perils of a brutal wilderness, often under the civilizing influence of a respectable girl from the East. But these were not the first dramatic works shot in Canada; that honour goes to Joe Rosenthal's '*Hiawatha*' *The Messiah of the Ojibway* (1903), made in Desbarats, Ontario, with a cast of Ojibway Indians.

By 1914 American film companies had discovered Canada and about 100 dramatic films had been made with Canadian content. From them was born a new genre, the 'northwoods melodrama' and its sub-genre the Mountie film. They were dramatized 'scenics', borrowing stereotypes from the emerging American Western. Sheriffs donned Mountie uniforms; cowboys became lumberjacks and prospectors; Mexican villains and servants became French Canadians; the ingredients were those of primitive melodrama—the 'race for life', the Indian attack, the heroine saved from death or worse—that typified pulp fiction, popular theatre, and American silent movies.

American interest in Canada did not stop at location shooting. Influential Americans were soon openly advocating the American takeover of the moving picture business in Canada. This expansionism coincided with the anti-American feeling preceding the 1911 Canadian election, which swept the Conservatives to power on a protectionist platform. By 1915 the new provincial film censorship boards, designed to protect minors and placate the Society for the Suppression of Vice, were banning gratuitous displays of the American flag in films. American interests would have to wait ten more years to complete their takeover.

In the meantime Canadian companies dedicated to the 'Canadian production of Canadian stories' began to sprout. As companies of convenience for American interests, they were registered in Canada and used Canadians in subsidiary roles before and behind the camera, but Americans in major roles. But Canada now became more than a scenic backdrop; the films used themes from Canadian history. In Montreal two Indian dramas were drawn from seventeenth-century Quebec history: *The Battle of the Long Sault*, (1913) and *Madeleine de Verchères* (1913). In Halifax, N.S. the Canadian Bioscope Company made *Evangeline* (1913)—the first dramatic feature- length film made in Canada—from the popular Longfellow poem recounting the Expulsion of the Acadians in 1755. Its success prompted six more dramas and comedies before Canadian Bioscope failed in 1914. In Windsor, Ont. the All-Red Feature Company produced *The War Pigeon* (1914), a love story set in the War of 1812, but despite an attempt at newsreel production, All-Red folded within a year. In Toronto the Conness Till Film Company released several films in early 1915, including a Mountie story, a war drama, and a comedy, all starring the Americans Edward Robins and Clara Whipple. Plans to film a series of Ralph Connor's novels died when fire destroyed the studios in late May.

This first inauthentic attempt to Canadianize the film industry—with American expertise, casts, and capital—was followed by an effort to launch major studio production in Trenton, Ont., by the Toronto promoter George Brownridge. After many ups and downs a company called Adanac released several films including *The Great Shadow* (1919), a Red-scare drama that apparently had the backing of the protectionist Canadian Reconstruction Association, and various large 'Employers of Labour'. But by 1920 Adanac too had drowned in a sea of debt and in 1924 the Trenton Studios were bought by the Ontario Government Motion Picture Bureau. Perhaps the future of Canadian film-making lay not in the studio system, but in the tradition of the early itinerant showmen.

THE SHIPMAN ERA 1919–23

The Canadian who briefly filled the bill was **Ernest Shipman**, a successful theatre and film impresario on both sides of the border. His entrepreneurial style consisted in arriving in a city, establishing a film company with local money for one or two films, and then moving on. In five years he did this in Calgary, Winnipeg, Ottawa, Sault Ste Marie, and Saint John. The approach favoured location shooting and avoided high studio overheads. For plots he chose popular fiction about pioneering life and adventure in the Canadian north, beginning with the prolific American writer of northwood romances, James Oliver Curwood. From one of his short stories, 'Wapi, the Walrus', came Canada's silent film classic, *Back to God's Country* (David Hartford, 1919), starring Ernie's wife **Nell Shipman** who is also credited with much of the work of adaptation and staging.

Back to God's Country is a curious amalgam of northern adventure and the romantic celebration of woman's oneness with nature. The melodramatic love triangle consists of the nymph-like Dolores (played by Nell Shipman), the villainous Rydal who tries to rape her and then kills her father, and Peter, the hero she marries and rescues from Rydal's attempts at revenge on an Arctic voyage. Curwood's story centred on the dog Wapi, but Nell expanded the woman's role in the rescue, and created the idyllic portrait of Dolores as nature-child, living in communion with nature in the northern forest. Critic Seth Feldman has linked this unspoken communion with what he calls the celebration of the silent subject in English-Canadian cinema; Peter Morris found it redolent of Northrop Frye's formulation of the pastoral myth in the Canadian imagination. But the film can be seen as projecting familiar stereotypes of women's relation to the world, isolated from the male-driven economy. Twice Dolores escapes from this dream-world when the language-bound men she loves (her politician-father, her writer-husband) are threatened by the villain cloaked in authority (Rydal appears first in the clothes of a Mountie he has killed, and later as the captain of the ship on which the couple embark). But when evil is overcome, Dolores returns to 'God's country', a parallel utopia that leaves the values of the secular City unchallenged.

With the Shipmans' divorce in 1920 the contract with Curwood lapsed. Nell left for the U.S. and a successful career as actress, screen-writer, and director, at a time when these last two professions included virtually no women at all. Ernie turned to Canadian author Ralph Connor for his next films. To direct them Shipman brought in Henry MacRae, a native of Stayner, Ontario, and 'king of the serial makers' at Universal City Studios. From Connor's novel *The Foreigner* (1909) came *God's Crucible* (1920), a melodrama of a struggle to overcome anti-immigrant prejudice; *Corporal Cameron of the North West Mounted Police* (1912) became a standard Mountie film, *Cameron of the Royal Mounted* (1921); *The Man from Glengarry* (1922) and *Glengarry School Days* (1922) were inspired by Connor's two most enduring works. Shipman next turned to a novel by Alan Sullivan: *The Rapids* (1922) was warmly received in Sault Ste Marie but tepidly elsewhere. One work by Halifax author Frederick William Wallace was shot, but it never gained release, even though it starred a young

Norma Shearer. As the Hollywood giants secured control of the industry, small independents like Shipman were eventually forced out.

Shipman's seven-film adventure was notable in several respects. He attempted independent production in Canada with an appeal to national sentiment and regional pride. His films elevated the status of location shooting from local colour to the integration of natural scenery and local history into the action. Contemporary critics found the feeling for landscape their best feature, just as a new school of landscape painting was emerging in Ontario's Laurentian shield. Shipman sought inspiration in a new home-grown popular fiction, just as 'the Americanization of the Canadian national image' (Pierre Berton's phrase) was proceeding apace in Hollywood. And although his films were exploited as action melodramas, some of them escaped the worst excesses of popular Hollywood genres.

OUIMET AND EARLY CANADIAN NEWSREELS

The earliest newsreel pioneer of substance in Canada was **Léo-Ernest Ouimet**. He had already made a reputation as a canny and successful theatre owner with his Ouimetoscopes. When he began making newsreels, his success at capturing the great news events of the day soon became legendary: the Quebec Bridge Disaster (1907), the Trois-Rivières fire (1908), Body Leach's successful descent of Niagara Falls in a barrel (1911), the aftermath of the sinking of the *Empress of Ireland* in the St Lawrence (1914), and the Halifax Explosion (1917). In the fashion of the time he reconstituted events when on-the-spot footage was lacking, as in *L'Affaire de la gare Windsor* (1909), about a train accident in Montreal, and in his version of the sinking of the *Titanic* (1912). In 1907 he included some of the new editing principles in a story-newsreel of an endurance race in the streets of Montreal, having set up a camera at different points along the course and in a moving car.

In 1915 Ouimet went into distribution with his own company, Specialty Film Import, and it was not long before he had two newsreel series feeding this distribution network from coast to coast. It was wartime and newsreels switched to propaganda. When Ouimet's cameramen joined up, they made films on training, combining actual events in a broader fictional or exemplary framework, anticipating later developments in Canadian documentary.

The end came slowly and sadly for Ouimet. Family calamities led to the collapse of his marriage in 1922. In the same year his newsreel network folded and Specialty Film Import was sold. Two years later most of the films in the Specialty collection were burnt. Ouimet, now in Hollywood, produced an unsuccessful comedy feature, *Why Get Married?* (Paul Cazeneuve, 1923), and plans for a production of *Maria Chapdelaine* came to nothing. By the mid-thirties Quebec's first great film impresario was working as a liquor-store manager.

Many of the first Canadian film-production companies, spurred on by Ouimet's early successes, also tried weekly newsreel production. Despite an attempted ban, wartime news coverage included longer patriotic compilations such as Conness Till's *Canada in Peace and War* (1915), and A.D. Kean's *B.C. for the Empire* (1916). But after the war two American companies began branch-plant newsreels—*Fox Canadian News* and *Canadian Kinograms*—which outlived all Canadian-made competitors. Local newsreel production went the way of the fiction film industry.

During the war, however, American influence had been seen as contrary to national interest. To protect those interests the only recourse lay in state film production, all the more appealing when it was clear that film offered the best channel of mass communication for government information.

EARLY GOVERNMENT PRODUCTION

In principle, wartime film production was co-ordinated from England. Although efforts were made to ban other war films, a six-reeler (*Canada's Fighting Forces*, 1915)—the life of 'Jack Canuck', from enlistment and training to the Front—was made by the official government photographer Lt. D.S. Dwyer. Actual hospital scenes were filmed, but no live shots of warfare: battles were described in diagrams. The Canadian government also sponsored films promoting war bonds at home and adapted similar American films to the Canadian context. There was even a Chaplin film called *The Bond*. But after trouble with the American company Essanay, all government film production was co-ordinated in 1917 under the dynamic leadership of

Bernard Norrish at Trade and Commerce. Over the next seven years, studios were built in Ottawa and a production schedule of ten shorts a year established. In 1924 the Canadian Government Motion Picture Bureau (CGMPB) under **Ray Peck** was established with a mandate to advertise abroad 'Canada's scenic attractions, agricultural resources and industrial development', to distribute Canadian pictures in Canada, and to help different regions get to know each other. 'Scenic attractions' soon became the dominant fare of the Bureau as Peck pursued theatrical distribution in the U.S. Peck also encouraged American companies to shoot on location in Canada and, although this policy was later dropped, it established the notion that Hollywood could play a role in promoting tourism in Canada.

In 1927, after Peck's death, Capt. **Frank Badgely** took over. A Canadian war veteran, Badgely had worked with D.W. Griffith in Hollywood, before returning to Ottawa to work as a film editor for the CGMPB. In his fourteen-year stint, while the social documentary developed in Britain and elsewhere, the Bureau continued turning out simple travelogues. John Grierson recalls that a friend remarked to him in 1931: 'If life in the Dominion is as these films represent, we might expect Canadians to engage only in fishing, golf and the observation of wild animals. There are practically no industries, very little work and no working people.'

Other government departments—notably the National Parks Bureau— were now making and circulating their own films. The best ones were made by **Bill Oliver**. Oliver's films featured nature conservation and natural adventure. Conservation is typified by the Grey Owl series, made with the English immigrant Archibald Stansfeld Belaney who gained international fame after adopting an Indian identity and living in the backwoods. The adventures include mountaineering films, and nature spectaculars featuring daring photography of wildlife in dangerous locations. Clearly a different breed from the makers of the first 'scenics', Oliver—like Booth in British Columbia and Tessier in Quebec—left the railroad tracks far behind him and entered into direct contact with nature.

Despite such competition, the CGMPB thrived in the twenties and produced its first feature, *In the Shadow of the Pole* (1928), about the Canadian Arctic Expedition of that year. International circulation was growing, when the coming of 'talkies' abruptly threatened the

CGMPB's market. Costly changes such as the adoption of the new non-theatrical 16-mm. gauge film coincided with the onset of the Depression, and yet the Bureau faced extinction unless funds were received for sound production. It was 1934 before they came. A full-length compilation history of Canadian armed forces in the Great War was chosen to 'baptize' the new sound equipment. The international success of *Lest We Forget* (1935) probably eased the decision to celebrate the unveiling of the Canadian Memorial at Vimy Ridge with a one-hour sound film, *Salute to Valour* (1937). But apart from such new ventures, Bureau productions, according to Charles Backhouse, 'continued to portray the same golden wheatfields, the same leaping salmon and tumbling waterfalls as in pre-sound days, except that now they were accompanied by spoken dialogue and music.'

In the meantime Provincial governments had moved into film production. Ontario's Motion Picture Bureau—designed to engage in 'educational work for farmers, school children, factory workers and other classes'—began in 1917 with **S.C. Johnston** as its first director. After six years of coping with the two Toronto companies handling the Bureau's work, the Bureau began making and distributing its own films. In 1924 the Government purchased Adanac's Trenton studios and for a while the Bureau's fortunes soared. In 1925 it had a library of 2,000 films and was distributing 1,500 reels of film per month. But a number of expensive mistakes left the Bureau in 1930 holding antiquated equipment and film stock. When Mitchell Hepburn's Liberals won the 1934 Ontario election on a platform of government cutbacks, the Bureau was scrapped. The Ontario Bureau made one full-length documentary drama, **John McLean French**'s *Cinderella of the Farms* (1931).

In Quebec, government production was not centralized into one department until much later. As early as 1920 **Joseph Morin**, at the Ministry of Agriculture, was using film for educational purposes, and other provincial ministries followed suit. But only in 1941 did the province co-ordinate its film-making services in *Le Service de Ciné-Photographie*. The Quebec government has maintained a film department ever since.

On the Prairies, Saskatchewan established the Motion Picture Branch of the Bureau of Publications in 1924 and made educational films for a while, although its best-known production was a film commissioned from Pathescope on the local Ukrainian population, *Nation Building in Saskatchewan: The Ukrainians* (**Dick Bird**, 1920). Dick Bird later made two memorable sponsored dramatic shorts in the 1930s: *This Generation* (1934) for the Saskatchewan Co-operative Wheat producers and *Youth Marches On* (1938) for the Oxford Group Movement.

Government departments in British Columbia used film for promotional purposes from 1908 to 1919, when the province established the Patriotic and Educational Film Service, headed by **May Watkis**, the first woman to head such an agency in Canada. Within a year provincial legislation required all theatres to include Film Service shorts in every program. However, with growing opposition from exhibitors and accusations of political bias from the opposition in the 1920 and 1924 provincial elections, production of the theatrical series 'Pacific Coast Scenics' soon ended and program requirements were no longer enforced.

ASSOCIATED SCREEN NEWS 1920–57

In 1920 **Bernard Norrish** was lured by Edward Beatty (president of CPR) into establishing Associated Screen News of Canada Ltd. (ASN) in Montreal, with CPR as majority shareholder. ASN's expansion was remarkable: it grew from a staff of two in 1920 to over one hundred by the end of the decade; it built its own laboratory and even took on work from the U.S. In 1926 ASN moved to new premises, and in 1936 it built one of the most modern sound stages in the world. However, Norrish, like Peck at CGMPB, believed there were practical limits to home-grown production. ASN concentrated on newsreels, theatrical shorts, and sponsored films, and in these fields it eclipsed CGMPB to become the dominant film-making force in Canada between the wars.

Norrish, who felt that Canadian news lacked international content, emulated Ouimet in developing contacts with external newsreel companies and when Ouimet ceased production with British Pathé News Norrish took over that operation too. Eventually ASN's only genuine competitor in Canadian news footage for the export market was Fox Movietone. With expansion, new people were brought in: Roy Tash, who joined in 1925, became famous for his films on the Dionne Quintuplets in the 1930s.

ASN's silent series of the 1920s, 'Kinograms', included travelogues publicizing places served by CPR trains and ships; wildlife documentaries (such as **Berton S. Moore**'s films on New Brunswick); coverage of events such as Canada's Diamond Jubilee and Royal Visits; and ethnographic films about native peoples. The series died with the coming of sound.

The major film-maker to emerge from ASN was **Gordon Sparling**, a University of Toronto graduate who had worked at both provincial and federal Picture Bureaux before joining ASN in 1932, where he launched the 'Canadian Cameos' series. From 1932 to 1954 eighty-five editions appeared on topics ranging from winter sports to lyrical nature films. Several of Bill Oliver's films for National Parks— notably the Grey Owl cycle—were re-edited and re-issued, including their greatest success, *Grey Owl's Little Brother* (1932). Sparling occasionally attempted a 'rhapsodic style', characterized by rhythmical editing set to music, special optical effects, and camera play. The best known was *Rhapsody in Two Languages* (1934), a lyrical portrait of Montreal following the recent international vogue for 'city symphony' films. By the end of the decade the cameo series was using colour, and stole a march on the CGMPB with its own unofficial film of the Royal Visit, *Royal Banners Over Ottawa* (1939).

At least a third of the ten-minute 'Canadian Cameos' dealt with tourism, sports, and recreation just as the earlier CPR scenics and the CGMPB films had done. Compilation films often dwelt on curiosities in the style of newspaper trivia corners. By all accounts, images of the Great Depression and the 'dirty thirties' were assiduously avoided, as snow scenes had been in the CPR scenics. Series of novelty shorts were not uncommon elsewhere, but the prominence of this one in the historical record is indicative of the sad state of Canadian film in the thirties.

THE COMING OF SOUND AND QUOTAS

The advent of sound was not welcomed unequivocally by the film industry. It spelt death to many a promising acting career, caused widespread lay-offs of theatre musicians, meant massive capital equipment costs for studios and theatres alike, and spawned a new technology (sound reproduction), a demand for new skills (such as dialogue-writing), and a new generation of technicians (such as sound recorders and editors). It caught the CGMPB off guard and helped kill off the Ontario Motion Picture Bureau. It finished ASN's first theatrical short series ('Kinograms'). In Canada, the arrival of sound coincided with the introduction of the British Empire quota on foreign films and with the completion of a big-budget fiasco, *Carry On, Sergeant*. These events stunted the development of a local and independent film industry in Canada just as support for such an initiative was rising again.

A firm of independent distributors in London and New York had set the *Carry On, Sergeant* project in motion. They came to Toronto in 1926 after winning a contract for world-wide distribution of the OGMPB's films, hoping to produce a major film to celebrate Canada's war experience. They hired a popular British war cartoonist, **Bruce Bairnsfather**, to make it. With a budget of $300,000 and the use of the Ontario Bureau's studios at Trenton, the film got under way. Scheduling errors, personality conflicts, and financial mismanagement—largely resulting from Bairnsfather's inexperience in studio production—bedevilled the project. Its final cost was half a million dollars. *Carry On, Sergeant* opened in a blaze of patriotic publicity at the Regent theatre in Toronto in November 1928, but the reviews were less ecstatic than the publicity. A controversy arose over a scene showing the hero, Sergeant Bob Mackay, momentarily forgetting his wife at home and succumbing 'to the wiles of an *estaminet* girl'. The uproar discouraged more widespread distribution and by Christmas the film had vanished from circulation; it apparently never opened outside Ontario. Years later the National Film Archive of Canada acquired the film and—with the help of Gordon Sparling, who had been an assistant director—reconstituted a copy that was finally shown nationally on CBC television fifty years after it first opened (scant comfort for those involved with the production at the time). By May 1929 the company went bankrupt and many would think twice before investing in major Canadian film production again. Broader markets were still elusive, and, ironically, the new British quota system did not improve matters.

To combat American dominance of the film industry, a number of countries—Britain and Australia among them—had by 1928 established quotas restricting the numbers of foreign-made films that could be shown in their theatres. The Canadian government, largely on the advice of Ray Peck at the CGMPB, did not move. Canadian feature-film production in the next decade was instead shaped by British legislation, which effectively encouraged branch-plants in Canada. Under the British system, films produced anywhere in the British Empire were allowed into Britain freely as long as British subjects dominated the payroll. This led to the 'quota quickies', usually low-budget 'B' films made by companies fronting for American financial interests to cash in on preferential treatment in the British market. Every loophole was explored—one film, at least, being turned down when the only British subject discovered in a starring role was a police dog called Silverstreak.

There were twenty-one 'quota quickies' in all. Fourteen came from two companies established in Victoria by British-born **Kenneth Bishop**. The films were all shot in less than a month, for budgets no higher than $65,000. Only the last of them—*Convicted*, whose cast included a teenager called Rita Hayworth—is still in circulation. The sole benefit to Canada from the British quota system was the money Columbia Pictures pumped into the Victoria economy at the height of the Depression. The films did not do well and hindered the development of a Canadian film industry and culture: cynical exploitation of the British quota laws in Canada led to the exclusion of films produced outside Britain when the legislation was reviewed and amended in 1938. Thereupon Hollywood packed its bags and left.

The two most memorable English-language films made in Canada between the wars were not really Canadian at all. The better known one is **Robert Flaherty**'s *Nanook of the North* (1922). Flaherty, the son of an American mining prospector, had already visited and casually filmed the Arctic when, with money from the Revillon fur company, he left for Port Harrison (now Inoucdjouac) on the Hudson Bay side of the Ungava peninsula. There he concentrated on one Inuit family in order to personalize for popular audiences the life of the indigenous Arctic peoples. This was the role of Nanook, who re-enacted for the camera the traditional activities of his people: walrus hunting, ice-fishing, iglu-building, etc. In doing so Nanook became an enduring icon of his culture, although he never survived to know this: he died of starvation on a hunting trip two years later.

As an ethnographic essay *Nanook of the North* is important in two respects. One is that the film-maker acted as a catalyst to the action he wanted to film. It has been argued that such directorial involvement distorts reality, which should be recorded dispassionately. Nevertheless, Flaherty's catalytic approach became central to many branches of the *cinéma-vérité* movement in the late fifties and stood in opposition to the empirical style of the period. The other important feature of *Nanook of the North* is its frank revelation of the film-making process itself. Flaherty retains moments when people signal their awareness of the camera; the framing of some long scenes does not conceal the implicit staging of the action. Later, in the films of Quebec's *cinéma-direct* style, the hand-held moving camera would draw attention to the re-framing of action and would inscribe the questing eye of the cameraman as subject in the film.

The second independent American film made north of the border was *The Viking* (1931), written and produced by **Varick Frissell**, who was still in his twenties. It was shot extensively on location, both for the ship-board scenes and for a dramatic trek across the ice-fields. Frissell boldly insisted on direct sound recording in order to achieve acoustic authenticity—a remarkable feat for Arctic location shooting, given the cumbersome sound equipment of the early talkies. The production ended in disaster when, in an attempt to secure additional footage, the ship was lost at sea and twenty-eight men, including Frissell, perished with her. The film opened in its original form in Toronto in May 1931.

But despite these two influential 'imports', the picture of Canadian film production between the wars is bleak. State production lacked imagination and funding; the private sector was dominated by Holly-wood and distorted by the British quota laws. The brave souls who persisted in trying to make films went beyond the confines of organized industry. Canadian amateurs of the period worked on extensive projects within their communities, without achieving a lasting reputation beyond them, although they too are an intrinsic part of Canadian film-making history.

ITINERANT AND LOCAL FILM-MAKERS OF THE THIRTIES

Probably many stories could be told of amateur film-makers who shouldered a camera and set off collecting images of their land and showing them to small communities, but their role in Canadian film history is marginal. The work of **Alfred Booth**, who toured British Columbia in the thirties shooting and screening scenes in villages, small settlements, and relief camps, is logged in Colin Browne's catalogue of B.C. film. However, the independents who worked the Quebec circuits played a larger part in the development of a local film culture—the only one for many people. There were less than half as many movie theatres in Quebec as in Ontario, and seventy per cent of the seats were in Montreal. Some regions, the Gaspé for one, had no theatres at all. Moreover, although Quebec was the only province to permit Sunday opening in the mid-thirties, it was also the only province to prohibit movie theatre attendance to minors, accompanied or not. Rural visits by itinerant projectionists and the parallel circuits organized through schools and parish community halls were the major vehicle for film culture in the province. Throughout Quebec in the thirties and forties many churchmen continued to ride the local circuits with their projectors and cans of film, as Picard and Paradis had done in the silent era. The central figures, however, were Albert Tessier in Trois-Rivières, and Maurice Proulx who is best known for his work in Abitibi.

Albert Tessier (1895–1976) was a historian and a teacher at the Seminary in Trois-Rivières. For him still photography and film were unique tools for promoting a sense of regional identity and local history. The sole maker, distributor, and exhibitor of his film work, he travelled the length and breadth of Quebec providing his own live commentary. Recent filmographies list seventy Tessier films made over a thirty-five-year period (1925–60). Many of them are now in the *cinémathèque* in Trois-Rivières. But the number of films does not do justice to his work, since Tessier often re-cut films from show to show; his film-shows were 'performances' rather than viewings of immutable material. Tessier himself calculated that he conducted over three thousand such showings, always appearing in person. In the words of Tessier's biographer, René Bouchard, Tessier's cinema was 'an epic celebration of the familiar, trying to confer on seemingly unobtrusive moments the greatness that he recognizes in them and which exerts influence in a community. This was a formulation of the principle of *cinéma-vérité*, or at least of the participatory camera, illustrating the relationship of man and his cultural environment.'

Working with a handheld camera and available light, Tessier neither directed nor posed his human subjects. His films, cobbled together from the mass of footage he accumulated, dwelt on farm people, child-rearing, spiritual values, and history as the Church saw them.

Maurice Proulx joined the faculty of the agricultural college at Sainte-Anne de la Pocatière in 1934, just as the policy of northern settlement was getting into high gear. He made some 37 films from 1934 to 1961, either for the Ministry of Agriculture or, from 1942 on, for the Quebec government's film agency, Le Service de Ciné-Photographie. They offer a more official version than Tessier's of the prevailing rural ideology. Proulx's documentaries on the Abitibi region (*En Pays neufs*, 1934–7 and *Sainte-Anne-de-Roquemaure*, 1942) and the Gaspé (*En Pays pittoresques*, 1938–9) combine a didactic tone with the atmosphere of a family album. In some shots the settlers even assemble to pose for the camera. The films promoted co-operative management and self-sufficiency, the importance of maintaining traditional crafts in a period of mechanization, and the intertwined institutions of family, church, and school. Recent scholars have pointed out that students of the Quiet Revolution's origins will find no hint in these films of the changes bubbling below the surface of Quebec in the forties and fifties. Nevertheless, because of the importance of Proulx's Abitibi settlement films as a historical record, Pierre Perrault used footage from them in his elegiac retrospective on that region, *Le Retour à La Terre* (1976).

Just as the ASN's *Canadian Cameos* stand out in English Canada's desert of 'quota quickies' and lacklustre government production, Quebec's circuit-riding priests of the Depression and the Duplessis era achieved prominence in a cultural context where French-language films were little known and French-Canadian film-making was otherwise non-existent.

2

DOCUMENTARY FILM IN ENGLISH SINCE 1939

While serving as personal secretary to Canadian High Commissioner Vincent Massey in the late thirties, Ross McLean met the British school of documentary film-makers and recommended that their leader, **John Grierson**, visit Canada and advise the government on new directions in film policy. Within eighteen months of the invitation Grierson had visited Canada, made his report, drafted legislation, seen it adopted, and become the first Film Commissioner of the National Film Board of Canada (NFB). As a Board it lay outside the Civil Service and, with Mackenzie King's support, Grierson assumed personal control. By 1941 the old Motion Picture Bureau had been folded directly into the Film Board, and Badgley left. With the war effort the State's film-making capacity flourished. From 1941 to 1945 the staff complement increased from fifty to over seven hundred.

Grierson knew the old Bureau and, although scornful of the quality of their films, he had admired their technical capacity and their solutions to problems of distribution. By war's end, with the expertise of Canadian administrators like Ross McLean and Donald Buchanan, he had consolidated and expanded the local non-theatrical networks: eighty-five rural circuits, each with a travelling projectionist on a monthly cycle; numerous industrial and trade union circuits; volunteer projection services in local community groups and service clubs; and twenty regional film libraries. To remedy the weaknesses on the production side he trained a new generation of Canadians, importing expertise from the British documentary school. Chief among these was **Stuart Legg** who took charge of theatrical production. Grierson encouraged international contact with visiting documentarists from other countries—Irving Jacoby, Joris Ivens, Henri Storck, Robert Flaherty, and Boris Kaufman, for example. Young Canadians were hired, not for their film-making experience, but if they showed an intellectual agility and background similar to Grierson's: Stanley Jackson, Tom Daly, James Beveridge, Donald Fraser, Sydney Newman, Morten Parker, Michael Spencer, Gudrun Bjerring (Parker), and Jane Marsh Beveridge. Grierson also turned to Canadians in the private sector, contracting out work to both the well-established Associated Screen News and a young Budge Crawley.

Grierson had enumerated four objectives for government film propaganda: national prestige, general information, trade publicity, and specific departmental information. The first meant getting films shown in commercial theatres—films with the punch and polish needed to secure audience attention alongside Hollywood features. Commercial preference for a steady supply of 'supporting program' favoured series production. This would be Legg's work. The other objectives were the business of non-theatrical distribution, for targeted audiences. Here, films had to provide limpid exposition and stimulate debate, sometimes by adding trailers that suggested possible directions for discussion. Programs for such films were rounded out by sing-along films and animated shorts.

In a climate of hagiographic reverence, Grierson has sometimes been given sole credit for building Canada's reputation as a world leader in documentary and animated film production. But the break with the past was not absolute. The roots of the NFB lay not only in British documentary but also in the mood of cultural nationalism and political reform that flourished in Canada between the wars, and in the growing interest in progressive communications policy that led to the creation of the Canadian Radio League, the Canadian Association for Adult Education, and the National Film Society (later the Canadian Film Institute). Pioneers in these fields were also prominent in the early NFB. There is also a negative side to Grierson's influence. Recently historians have recalled Grierson's rejection of ideas for a Canadian commercial film industry, even when it meant fudging NFB attendance figures to win his point; his willingness to compromise his beliefs in dealings with government; his paternalistic treatment of women and women's issues; his carelessness of people's feelings.

The wartime documentary style he promoted has been called the imposition of the British imperial voice.

Nevertheless, Grierson's philosophy of documentary film and state production profoundly influenced the subsequent development of the NFB. In calling for the 'creative treatment of actuality' in film, Grierson raised a duel agenda of empirical observation and self-conscious purpose to the status of moral imperative. The film-making process should include moments of recording *and* construction. If Grierson often called his movement 'anti-aesthetic', this did not mean he rejected formal concerns. Rather he meant that the traces of the observed world recorded on films should be organized according to principles that had *both* an aesthetic *and* a social dimension. His repertoire of structural principles consisted of the *dramatic*, characterized by tensions and conflict (he cited Flaherty's films), the *symphonic*, characterized by movement and rhythm (the city 'symphonies'), and the *poetic*, characterized by the imagistic, the symbolic, and the connotative (Grierson's own *Drifters*, 1929). By stressing social purpose, Grierson wanted film to become a buttress of modern democracy, helping to build an informed citizenry as the foundation of progressive political development, in an age when communications technology encouraged social interdependence and collective enterprise. The appropriate instrument for such film-making was the State—not simply the government of the day, but a progressive public service organized according to the principle of the 'general sanction', that is, the limits of tolerable social change across the range of dominant partisan interests. The 'general sanction' has often bedevilled the NFB since, notably whenever its films appeared partisan, provided a vigorous critique of the political status quo, or seemed to endorse revolutionary politics or Quebec independence.

While Grierson filled the role of philosopher and advocate, it was **Stuart Legg** who provided leadership in creating the new style on film. His first NFB films on youth training schemes made before the war—*Youth is Tomorrow* (1939) and *The Case of Charlie Gordon* (1939)—represent two distinct approaches: the former a macrocosmic, dialectical statement of the problem through a *symphonic* montage of images in three parts (productive youth, unemployed youth, and youth in training) similar to the CGMPB's *Heritage* (J. Booth Scott, 1939), a thirty-minute epic of the prairie from buffalo to dust bowl and on to recovery; the latter a microscosmic, *dramatic* exposition of one case-history, with exemplar and cycle as in the British classics *Drifters* (1929) and *Night Mail* (1936).

From the war years, the most memorable films are from Legg's two theatrical series: *Canada Carries On* (*CCO*, 1940–59) and *The World In Action* (*WIA*, 1942–45). Never more than twenty minutes long, they presented images of Canada's war effort and its geopolitical context, grounded in Legg's inspirational commentary—delivered with deep, reassuring authority by Lorne Greene—which was laid over the densely orchestrated music of Lucio Agostini and, later, Louis Applebaum. The two series are not as easy to distinguish as their titles suggest, but *WIA* was launched with the aim of adopting the geopolitical perspective of some *CCO* films in the first two years. Some *CCO* films featured specially shot footage and the dramatic action or case-history format; others and almost all *WIA* films were skilful compilations by Legg and Tom Daly of acquired footage. The stress on compilation offered full play to the faculties of selection and sequencing in constructing the final work, but rare opportunities for the sensitive and purposive observation so often cited as a hallmark of NFB films. Moroeover, the speed of production—the Board had 'to bang them out one a fortnight and no misses', as Grierson put it—compromised the organic development of the film story 'taken from the location' that was implicit in the Flaherty tradition. Nevertheless, the films attracted considerable international attention to the new NFB, and their treatment of the Battle of Britain, *Churchill's Island* (*CCO*, June 1941), won the first Oscar awarded in the short documentary category.

Sidney Newman and **Guy Glover** continued the *CCO* series after Legg moved over to *WIA* . When possible they made films of process-cycles in the British tradition, using rhythmical editing and compositional patterns to build symphonic form—*Trans-Canada Express*, (*CCO*, April 1944), for example. **Tom Daly**, Legg's earlier assistant, made films on northern manœuvres whose editing patterns articulated a rise and fall of tension (*Ordeal by Ice*, *CCO* ,1945), and he was first to include images of the Holocaust: *Guilty Men* (*WIA* ,1945), an analysis of war crimes tribunals.

Similar films promoting the war effort were being made for non-theatrical circuits. Some were stripped-down versions of the theatrical films, but more often they were openly didactic and less attentive to the showmanship required to command interest in theatres. The 'Knife and Fork' films dealt with food and nutrition. Others promoted government services, such as the mail, day-nurseries, Labour-Management Production Committees, and Unemployment Insurance—*A Man and His Job* (Dallas Jones, 1943) used the case-history approach. There were six different newsreel series, targeting specific audiences (rural, industrial, military). To help Canadians know each other better there were films on regional and ethnic minorities and native peoples. Unfortunately such films had a tendency to patronize and stereotype. The symphonic approach reasserted itself in *Peoples of Canada*, made by ASN's Gordon Sparling and later revised by Legg for inclusion in *CCO* (March 1941), but its images of Quebec bespoke only the seasonal round, the country soil, and the parish church. The urban symphonist of Montreal (Sparling) and the social realist graduate from the GPO Film Unit (Legg) fell for the old Establishment view of Quebec. **Jane Marsh**'s *Alexis Tremblay, Habitant* (1943; French version *Terre de nos aïeux*) was another pastoral celebration—of the North Shore in Charlevoix county—an example of the 'picturesque' approach the French Unit film-makers would reject two decades later as the outsider's view.

Robert Flaherty also worked with the Board as a consultant to **Laura Boulton** on the first of her two films about native peoples, the realistic *Eskimos of the Eastern Arctic* (1944) and her more sentimental *People of the Potlatch* (1944). Finally, over the war years a number of 16-mm colour films were made for the NFB by **Budge Crawley, Graham McInnes**, and **Grant Crabtree**. They constituted the first 'Canadian Artists' series (1941–46) and two, in the native pastoral tradition—*Canadian Landscape* (Crawley, 1941), on A.Y. Jackson, and *West Wind* (McInnes, 1942), on Tom Thompson—portray an intimate, harmonious relationship between artist, nature, and community.

THE NFB FROM COLD WAR TO TELEVISION

Grierson always intended to leave the Board at the end of the War, yielding control to the Canadian film-makers nurtured within it. Accordingly, when Japan surrendered in 1945 Grierson resigned and many of the British team soon followed. Grierson's legacy to Canada was one of the world's largest film studios and a band of well-trained, innovative documentarists and animators making over a hundred films a year for commercial theatres and for non-theatrical programs supported by an intricate distributional network. The NFB model of State production would be copied in New Zealand, Australia, and South Africa.

When Stuart Legg left the Board, he expressed the hope that the Board would retain links with all sectors of the Canadian public, using documentary as 'a compass in the midst of change', continuing technical experimentation, and maintaining a supra-national perspective. Legg's hopes nearly failed to survive the aftermath of the Gouzenko affair of 1945–6. Among the revelations of Soviet defector Igor Gouzenko was the implication of one of Grierson's secretaries in a spy network. The Conservatives taunted the Liberal government about subversive tendencies in the NFB, as well as financial waste and government monopoly. Despite massive cuts after the war, the House of Commons rang with calls for more. By the late 1940s the position of the beleaguered NFB had become critical. The Massey Commission was reviewing government arts funding policy, a management-consultant firm was examining the NFB's administration, and the RCMP was screening Board employees as security risks. In Quebec the Duplessis government effectively banned NFB films from circulation. And when Grierson's successor, Ross McLean, spoke out for the NFB in 1949, a new Commissioner was brought in: **Arthur Irwin**, the editor of *MacLean's Magazine*. He was greeted at the Board with the reception usually reserved for public executioners.

But the Board's worst fears were not realized. The management report and the Massey Commission recommended expansion of the NFB. The RCMP screening claimed only three dismissals from a complement of 580. A new National Film Act stabilized the NFB's operations and budgets and reduced the possibility of political interference. Post-war cuts in distribution were offset by the sprouting of local networks under school boards, provincial government departments, wheat pools, community film councils, and so on. The National Film Society and the Canadian Educational Association sponsored specialized collections of NFB material and prepared guidebooks on their use in schools and elsewhere. In the Irwin years (1950–53) production and circulation rose steadily. International awards multiplied, culminating in the 1952 grand slam—a British Film Academy Award for best documentary (*Royal Journey*, David Bairstow 1951), an award at Cannes for best animated short (*Romance of Transportation in Canada*, Colin Low, 1952), and an Oscar for Norman McLaren's pixillated film *Neighbours* (1952). The aftermath of the Red Scare lay more in self-censorship and in-house editorial control than in political censorship and crippling cutbacks.

But the most successful NFB film under Irwin was the old stand-by, a royal tour. Ceremony and spectacle won out against narrative and illustration. **David Bairstow**'s *Royal Journey* (1951)—Princess Elizabeth and the Duke of Edinburgh—became a box-office record-breaker in Canada and went on its own successful tour of some forty countries. The previous government-made film of this length had been *The Royal Visit* (1939), Badgeley's final bow before the CGMPB was absorbed by the NFB. Bairstow's royal tour film silenced many of the NFB's detractors. Passage of the 1952 Board estimates in the House of Commons took ten minutes.

The films of this period showed many of the tendencies shown in the Grierson-Legg years and before. The case-history film with a problem-solving outline was used to present post-war social programs, as in **Grant McLean**'s award-winning *Farewell to Oak Street* (1953), on public housing in Toronto. Trade and tourism remained a central focus with films like *Fashions by Canada* (1946) and *Famous Fish I have Met* (1949). The so-called 'native style', the lyrical documentary, now more observational, flourished in films celebrating the land and the arts as in **Gudrun Bjerring Parker**'s *Listen to the Prairies* (1945).

The post-war trend to neo-realism, centred in war-torn Europe, focused attention on ways to integrate documentary and fiction. In Canada, it came to dominate documentary practice. Dramatized sequences were used in training films by **Robert Anderson** and **Stanley Jackson** like the 'Mental Mechanisms' series (1948–50) and its sequel 'Mental Symptoms' (1951), and worked so well that the films became minor classics and circulated widely. Dramatized case-histories were used in other films by Anderson and Jackson as well as *The Son* (Julian Biggs, 1951), on the difficulties of the family farm, and *Opera School* (Gudrun Parker, 1951), on the rise of a fictional opera singer from training to public performance. Most notable of all was *File 1365—The Connors Case* (**Donald Mulholland**, 1947), the re-enactment of an RCMP investigation and manhunt following a murder—ironic in light of the police investigation of the NFB under way at the time. Mulholland and Bairstow's five-part 'Accidents Don't Happen' (1946–49) dramatized accidents in the workplace, often with comic effect and voice-over commentary by Bernard Braden.

These dramatized documentaries were written and staged using the conventions of Hollywood editing and *mise-en-scène*, but they were shot in identifiable locations rather than studios. The actors were non-professionals, even painfully so. Some re-enacted their own experiences. When used, voice-over commentary dominated, generalizing from the particular. Rare were completely fictional works like the stilted children's comedy, *The Boy Who Stopped Niagara* (Leslie McFarlane, 1947).

In 1952 home-grown television came to Canada, and although the NFB had been selling films to its British and American predecessors, the arrival of CBC-TV meant the NFB now had to adapt to the demands of TV programming: tight modular scheduling, regular production, and running series—like the wartime theatrical series, but with two differences: no war to provide thematic continuity, and no need to rely on compilation of acquired footage. 'On the Spot' (1953–55), **Bernard Devlin**'s weekly series of film reportages for TV, required speed, economy, and ingenuity. Each program had to be researched, shot, and edited in a week for a tenth of the normal NFB budget. With commentator Fred Davis and a crew of only two (camera and sound), Devlin experimented. The new 16 mm. Auricon camera recorded sound directly on the film; more selection and sequencing decisions could now be made while shooting, and fewer while editing. The rough, improvised edge this gave to the film enhanced the sense of immediacy and authenticity. A good example is *Survival in the Bush* (1954), which combined the real-life experience of the film crew in a remote survival exercise with the didactic exposition of the participating expert.

The techniques and equipment of 'On the Spot' were used in the weekly docudrama series 'Perspective' (1955–58), in which such scriptwriters as Charles Israel and William Weintraub researched topical social issues and turned them into short, illustrative dramas. Directed by Stanley Jackson, Don Haldane, Donald Wilder, and producers Julian Biggs and Devlin themselves, they often adopted the case-history structure; some had on-camera expert commentary. John Foster on camera and John Locke on sound gave continuity of style to the series. Two of the films won CFAs: *Monkey on the Back* (Biggs, 1956), a tough story of a heroin addict's life and death, and *Saskatchewan Traveller* (Haldane, 1956), showing an ageing travelling salesman on the prairies and his trainee whose new ideas create tensions between them. However, the speed and volume of production led other films to descend into tiresome preaching.

As TV matured and the possibility of serious geopolitical analysis returned to the NFB, a new series of 'World in Action' (1957–60) got under way, with a return to compilation and the voice of authority. But now the films were grouped in sub-series, like chapters in a longer study, as in the thirteen-part 'The Commonwealth of Nations' (Ronald Dick, 1957); the prize-winning 'Women on the March' (Douglas Tunstell, 1958), a history of the suffragette movement; and 'Between Two Wars' (William Weintraub, 1960), a history of Canada from 1919 to 1939. Although ostensibly shot as documentary shorts, these series offered their makers the opportunity to make works that rivalled or surpassed the full-length features the Board would not fund out of deference to the private sector. Nevertheless, each edition could be seen and understood individually, and in some ways the series foreshadowed the travelling-historian shows that now dominate TV documentary, as in **John McGreevy's** work on 'Cities' (1976–79) and 'Peter Ustinov's Russia' (1985), **Gwynne Dyer**'s 'War' (1983), and so on.

With the expansion of documentary dramatization and a revival of the synthesizing compilation film, it might be assumed that the observational style was receding in prominence. There was, however, a lively group of talented young turks in Tom Daly's Unit B.

THE FILMS OF UNIT B

The core group of Unit B consisted of **Tom Daly** (producer), **Wolf Koenig**, **Roman Kroitor**, **Colin Low**, and, later, **Terence Macartney-Filgate**. They began work in the 1950s and continued together until the NFB replaced the units by the looser Pool system. The films of this tightly-knit group of intellectuals have attracted much critical attention. Peter Harcourt described the detached, contemplative quality of the commentaries and the poetic quality of the images. D. B. Jones emphasized the 'wholeness' of their work, which celebrated coherence in the world through coherent form. Bruce Elder dwelt on their end-of-ideology empiricism. Unit B rejected the trend towards docudrama but did not return to the certainties of the Griersonian style. They admired French photographer Henri Cartier-Bresson and the new British documentary movement of the fifties (the 'Free Cinema' of Lindsay Anderson, Karel Reisz, and Tony Richardson). They yearned for authenticity in place of authority and sought the point of intersection between truth and beauty in the Romantic tradition.

The empirical tendency emerged in two early ten-minute films: *Paul Tomkowitz: Street Railway Switchman* (Kroitor, 1954), a wistful, subtle portrait of a Polish immigrant in his twenty-third year of maintaining streetcar rails in Winnipeg; and *Corral* (Low, 1954), a lyrical demonstration of the crucial stages of breaking a range horse leading to saddling and first mount. In these films, there was no overt didactic message, and no social injustice requiring or obtaining redress. The words of Tomkowitz are heard over the sounds of his work and images of wintry evenings on the tracks; the gestures of horse-breaking are observed without comment over Eldon Rathburn's evocative score for two guitars. Instances of human life 'speak for themselves'. The trend was pushed further with the fourteen shorts of the 'Candid-Eye' series (1958–59). A detached, ironic observer registers surface impressions of a myth-laden aspect of Canadian life, in order to de-mythicize and de-dramatize it but without analysis or critique. The pilot *The Days Before Christmas* (Macartney-Filgate *et al.*, 1958) showed Montreal's pre-Christmas rush, shot extemporaneously by several cameramen working without a script. *Blood and Fire* (Macartney-Filgate, 1958) gave an inside view of the work of the Salvation Army; *I Was a Ninety-Pound Weakling* (Wolf Koenig and Georges Dufaux, 1959) was an ironic and still topical portrayal of health clubs; and *The Back-Breaking Leaf* (Macartney-Filgate, 1959) showed life in the Ontario tobacco fields. The culmination of the Unit B's naïve observer films was the later *Lonely Boy* (Koenig and Kroitor, 1961), showing a few days in the life of the singing idol Paul Anka. It was showered with prizes, including Canadian Film of the Year in 1963, the third Unit B film to be so honoured. The film emphasized its uncontrolled shooting style by retaining sequences where people alluded to it.

The speculative strand emerged in *City of Gold* (Low & Koenig, 1957), a meditation on the Klondike Gold Rush of 1897, using glass slides from the period, a commentary of personal reflections by Pierre Berton who grew up there, and another connotative musical score by Rathburn. Berton revised American-inspired images of the Gold Rush and probed the motives and feelings of the men who undertook the journey. As he did so, the distorting legend was supplanted not by another certainty but by a sense of reflection and uncertainty. The film bracketed the central portion—pans over still photographs of the era—by live-action shots of present-day Dawson, a ghost of its former self. This structure has been interpreted as a nostalgic longing for the past, or linked to a distinctively Canadian preoccupation with the transfiguration of the photographic image through filmic presentation. But *City of Gold* stands also as a paradigm of the Romantic dream-journey cycle. A quiet setting (present-day Dawson) provokes an imaginary voyage of discovery (the exploratory contemplation of traces of a stirring past) from which the dreamer awakes to a sense of loss and tranquil reflection. This pattern also echoes both the experience of the documentary investigator, whose questing eye is represented in the slow pans across the old slides, and the experience of the spectator, entering the dark to share this exploration before returning to the real world. But if the cyclical structure of the film implies closure, the voice we hear does not. The explorer returns, not with pockets lined with new certainty, but 'enriched' with a sense of ineffable wonder and unresolved mystery. The process is closed and clear, the product is elusive and vague.

This combination of dream-journey-cycle and unresolved mystery recurred in the sixties, most notably in *Universe* (Low & Kroitor, 1960) and their series for Expo '67 in Montreal, *Labyrinth* (Kroitor & Low, 1967). In *Universe*, the cycle was an astronomer's visit to the David Dunlap Observatory near Toronto, enhanced by Rathburn's score and Wally Gentleman's special effects that anticipate his work on Stanley Kubrick's *2001, A Space Odyssey* (1968). In the Labyrinth films, the journey was undertaken by the audience literally, as they moved through a structure of events of which films were only a part. Spectators in balconies watched the human life cycle on two wide screens, one vertical on the wall, one horizontal on the floor, before going through the labyrinthine passages to a symbolic encounter with the 'Minotaur', arranged on five screens forming a cross. The conjunction of the candid style (of the improvised shooting), speculative humanism, and technical experimentation were synthesized in this, the swan song of the Unit B team.

THE POOL SYSTEM AND THE GROWTH OF THE PERSONAL STYLE

Although the unit system suited the like-minded co-operative spirit of the Unit B documentarists, other film-makers felt imprisoned in their units. In 1964 the Board responded by instituting a Pool system in the English language branch. Directors now brought project proposals to a committee for approval before choosing a producer from the pool. Since the initiative now passed from administrator to film-maker, individual creativity could be encouraged, in keeping with the growing interest in the artistic role of the director as *auteur*. The years of the Pool system (1964–71) saw the advent of new directors, an emphasis on personal work, and self-referentiality. The new generation was typified by Donald Brittain, Michael Rubbo, Martin Duckworth, Bill Mason, and others who emerged at this time.

Donald Brittain felt affinities with Unit B but only worked with them when he co-wrote *Labyrinth* (Kroitor & Low, 1964–67). His subjects have included war, most notably *Memorandum* (1965), on the Holocaust; biographies, especially the three-part series 'The Champions' (1978 & 1986), on Pierre Trudeau and René Lévesque; and in *Canada's Sweetheart* (1985), on the corrupt union leader Hal Banks, he mixed interview-reminiscence and dramatized reconstructions. With his early history of Canada's film industry (*Dreamland*, 1974), and his studies of bureaucracy (*Paperland: the Bureaucrat Observed* ,1979) and the world of the modern spy ('On Guard for Thee' series, 1981), Brittain established himself as the best of NFB's narrative historians. In his judicious editing and rhetorical commentary, he often recalls Stuart Legg. His personal stamp comes from a tone of ironic detachment, ocasional black humour, a feel for curious juxtapositions, and a sense of scale and context. The individuality of Brittain's work emerges when his tart historical narratives are compared to the observational, uncritical portrait of *'Dief'* (1981) by **Bill**

Canning, in which archival footage of Diefenbaker's witticisms and oratory are inserted without comment into shots of his funeral.

If Brittain's films emphasize and extend the ironic distance of the Unit B team, those of **Michael Rubbo** emphasize and extend Unit B's epistemological uncertainties and self-reflexive tendencies. Rubbo's films highlight his presence as speculative participant and his own voice-over often reveals his doubts about the value of his interpretations. He recounts his contact as an outsider with societies in flux around the world: daily life in wartime Vietnam (*Sad Song of Yellow Skin*, 1970), a visit to Indonesia (*Wet Earth and Warm People*, 1971), or a trip round Cuba with two Canadian politicians (*Waiting for Fidel*, 1974). In Canada he chose times of intense political activity—anti-pollution campaigns (*Persistent and Finagling*, 1971), the 1976 Quebec election (*I Hate to Lose*, 1977), or its subsequent independence referendum (*Yes or No, Jean-Guy Moreau*, 1979)—and concentrated on the elusive feelings, the ambiguous identities, and the sense of isolation of those caught up in the process, images that confirm and reflect his own ambiguous status as participant-observer.

The films of **Martin Duckworth** span many familiar NFB trends and preoccupations: social documentaries and direct cinema reportage on prison life, coal-mining in Cape Breton, a mill closure in Quebec, and the international peace movement. But two personal films illustrate the Pool system aesthetic. *The Wish* (1970) shows Duckworth's two daughters returning to the family homestead in Quebec and *Accident* (1973) relives a fatal small plane crash from which the cameraman shooting at the time survived. **Bill Mason** celebrates the natural world in a strongly personal way, particularly in his films on canoeing and wolves. *Cry of the Wild* (1971) incorporated diary sequences about the making of the film. And for comparison, Bill Canning's film on mountains, the Etrog-winning *Temples of Time* (1971), once again illustrates the lyrical style.

CHALLENGE FOR CHANGE AND DECENTRALIZATION

In the late 1960s climate of participatory democracy, a number of alternative modes and uses of cinema were being attempted and the NFB followed suit. The Challenge for Change program (1967–80), under the impetus of Colin Low, aimed to transform the NFB practice of making films sponsored by Government Departments into two-way communication. D. B. Jones distinguished three distinct kinds of film project in the series. The first, which drew inspiration from an earlier *The Things I Cannot Change* (Tanya Ballantyne, 1966), a living documentary on a poor Montreal family, articulated a social problem to the general public. The second was designed to stimulate debate among 'change-agents', as in Bonnie Sherr Klein's films on the community organizing of Saul Alinsky. The third and major category consisted of films made within a deprived or marginal community to help it communicate its own concerns to other similar communities or to appropriate policy-makers. Such was Colin Low's *Fogo Island* project (1967), some twenty-eight short films made among the isolated peoples off the north-east coast of Newfoundland threatened by government resettlement. The film-makers did not intervene in the action and they allowed the community final say about the content of the films.

Grierson, visiting in Canada, was skeptical, feeling the approach miniaturized issues and did not constitute true decentralization; this would come only if local groups were trained to make their own films. And indeed this kind of decentralization took place, as the Challenge for Change participatory approach made way for local film-makers, with native peoples' programs, multiculturalism, and regionalization.

The 'Netsilik Eskimos' series (1967) on the Inuit of Pelly Bay and the 'Challenge for Change' films by **Boyce Richardson** and **Tony Ianzelo** made with the Cree Indians of the James Bay region—*Cree Hunters of the Mistassini* (1974) and *Our Land Is Our Life* (1974)—followed the participatory model, but native film-makers have been making their own since Michael Mitchell made *These Are My People* (1969), with the first Indian film crew. Most prominent has been **Alanis Obomsawin**, with *Amisk* (1977), built around a native concert in support of the Mistassini Cree; *Mother of Many Children* (1977), an 'album of native womanhood'; *Incident at Restigouche* (1984), documenting a fishing rights confrontation between the Quebec police and the Micmac people; and most recently the harrowing *Richard Cardinal: Cry from a Diary of a Métis Child* (1986), on a case-history of teenage suicide. Similarly, recent immigrant communities have undertaken to film their own testimony. Such films have often drawn on the personal world of the film-maker, as in Tony Ianzelo's *Antonio* (1966), on his Italian father; **Harvey Spak**'s *Pamiat, Memory of Ancestors* (1981), about his Ukrainian grandparents' settlement in Saskatchewan; or **David Troster**'s independently made *Bubbie* (1978, distributed by the NFB), on his Jewish grandmother in Toronto's Spadina district.

In the seventies, building on the experience of an earlier Vancouver Film Unit, NFB Regional Production Centres or Studios were added in Halifax, Winnipeg, Toronto, and Edmonton. Their mandate was not only to make films with regional content but to nurture a local film community. Their films often resemble regional journalism or television, celebrating native sons and daughters, compiling local histories, investigating local issues, viewing the local economy. The desire to avoid the national perspective, identified as a central Canadian metropolitan view, has led to conflicts between the NFB's 'house' style and the aspirations of local directors anxious to acquire a distinct identity. Nevertheless regional film-makers as yet unrecognized in the film encyclopedias of central Canada have emerged: in the Atlantic Studio, **Kent Martin** and **Brian Pollard**; in the Prairie Studio, **Norma Bailey** and **Robert Lower**; in the Pacific Studio, **Moira Simpson** and **Larry Kurnarsky**. Others made NFB regional documentaries before making fictional features: **Bill MacGillivray** in the Atlantic Studio; **Tom Shandel** and **Phillip Borsos** (*Nails*, 1979) in the Pacific Studio; **Anne Wheeler** in both the Pacific Studio (*Augusta*, 1976) and at the North West Studio (*A War Story* ,1981).

STUDIO D AND OTHERS

In 1971 the Board introduced a system of Studios, a looser form of Units that facilitated mobility and voluntary affiliation, while restoring the cohesion it was felt the Pool system had lost. Best known is Studio D, even though it was not formed until 1974. The stimulus for a special focus on women's issues came from the upcoming International Women's Year in 1975, although series on women had been made in the 'Challenge for Change' program: 'En tant que femmes' (1973–74) and 'Working Mothers' (1974–75). **Kathleen Shannon**, the producer-director of 'Working Mothers', headed Studio D until 1987 as the NFB's first woman executive producer. In thirteen years the Studio has established itself as a major force in the women's movement in Canada. Its films provoke community discussions on a scale that recalls the heady Grierson days, and its three Oscars catapulted it into international prominence: *I'll Find a Way* (**Beverly Shaffer**, 1977), about a lively handicapped girl, *If You Love This Planet* (**Terri Nash**, 1982), based on Helen Caldecott's powerful appeal for nuclear disarmament, and *Flamenco at 5.15* (**Cynthia Scott**, 1983), on the Robledos' flamenco class at the National Ballet School. Its films often focus attention on exemplary women: in new roles (*I Want to be an Engineer*, Beverly Shaffer, 1983); as artists and writers in *Portrait of the Artist—as an Old Lady* (**Gail Singer**, 1982) and the feature *Firewords* (**Dorothy Todd Hénaut**, 1987); as agents of change in *The Lady from Grey County* (**Janice Brown**, 1977), on Agnes McPhail, Canada's first woman MP, in *Dream of a Free Country* (Shannon & Stikeman, 1983), on women activists in Nicaragua, and in *Speaking Our Peace* (Terri Nash and Bonnie Klein, 1985), on women in the international peace movement. Sex-role stereotyping was probed in a compilation of the NFB's own work in the series 'How They Saw Us' (**Ann Pearson**, 1977). Controversial themes have tested the 'general sanction', but were close to the heart of the women's movement: pornography in *Not a Love Story* (Bonnie Klein, 1981), abortion in *Abortion: Stories from North and South* (Gail Singer, 1984), and women in the church, in *Behind the Veil: Nuns* (**Margaret Westcott**, 1984).

A final word about some some current NFB work and its most recent generation of film-makers. **Paul Cowan** came to prominence in the late seventies with a number of films on sports and athletics, one of which, *Going the Distance* (1979), won an Oscar nomination. However, he is better known now for the controversy sparked by *The Kid Who Couldn't Miss* (1982), a mixture of documentary sources and staged re-enactments scrutinizing the legend of First World War flying hero Billy Bishop that prompted a Senate enquiry from out-raged veterans. Cowan used a similar mixture in *Democracy on Trial: The Morgentaler Affair* (1984) to show Dr Henry Morgentaler's recent challenge to abortion laws through the Quebec courts. **Albert Kish**, a Hungarian immigrant, has been active in making films celebrating multi-culturalism—*Our Street Was Paved with Gold* (1973), *Bekevar Jubilee* (1977), and *Hold the Ketchup* (1977)—and has explored the mediation of experience and memory through various modes of representation in *The Age of Invention* (1984), on the years before the first World War, and in *Los Canadienses* (1975), on Canadians in the Spanish Civil War. These two interests came together in his *This Is a Photograph* (1971), which won two **CFA**s. The NFB's symbiotic relationship with other performing arts in Canada is illustrated in much of the work by both **John N. Smith** and **Cynthia Scott**, who worked together on *For Love of Dance* (1981) and the feature-length *Gala* (1982). Smith is better known for his Oscar-winning dramatization *First Winter* (1981), about an Irish family arriving to settle in the Ottawa Valley in 1830. Finally, the tradition of unbridled direct cinema persists in the sensational *Final Offer* (Sturla Gunnarsson & Robert Collison, 1986), in which the film-makers captured in raw detail union negotiators during the 1984 UAW—General Motors contract talks that led to the creation of the new Canadian Auto Workers union under its charismatic leader, Bob White.

DOCUMENTARY BEYOND THE NFB

Such is the scale, reputation, and accessibility of the National Film Board, that historians inevitably give less attention to commercial and independent documentaries. The most important maker of sponsored films was Crawley Films. **F.R. Budge Crawley** and **Judith Crawley** incorporated their company in 1946, having taken on contract work for the NFB during the war. During the next thirty-five years they produced over 2,500 films and won more than 200 awards. The first two Canadian Film of the Year awards went to them for *The Loon's Necklace* (1948), which told an Indian legend using B.C. Indian masks, and *Newfoundland Scene* (1951), a documentary made upon Newfoundland's entry into Confederation. Despite its increasing interest in financing Canadian feature dramas, the company returned to prominence in the seventies with the documentary compilation features *Janis* (Howard Alk & Seaton Findlay, 1974, **CFA**) and *The Man Who Skied Down Everest* (Judith Crawley, 1975, Oscar).

Other husband-and-wife companies are Chetwynd, founded in 1950 by Sir **Arthur Chetwynd** and his wife **Marjorie**. Sports films account for about a third of their more than 3,000 sponsored and educational films, of which a dozen or so have won **CFA**s, but their work never matched the Crawleys' best. **Lawrence Cherry** (1900–66) and **Evelyn Spice Cherry** (1900–), whose careers had taken them to Grierson's GPO Film Unit in Britain, the NFB's Agricultural Unit and a Saskatchewan Film Unit, finally set up Cherry Film Productions in 1961 in Regina and made educational film series for the Saskatchewan government. Sunrise Films, based in Toronto, was founded by **Paul** and **Deepa Saltzman** in 1973, and has specialized in films for television showing the inspirational daily life and work of people around the world.

Other initiatives have come from co-operatives and private groups, by their nature more fragile and changeable. In the early seventies film production co-operatives sprang up in almost every province. Alongside documentarists, they also attracted experimentalists and some formed excellent animation branches, although the dream of fictional features remained the sustaining focal point for many. The Toronto Co-op, the largest and earliest, disbanded in the wake of divisions between experimentalists and aspirants to the commercial mainstream. Filmwest Associates, a looser co-operative in Edmonton, subdivided several times as the film industry grew in Alberta. Independent companies were often formed in large television centres by freelancers branching out from the CBC, the NFB, or larger private corporations like Moreland-Latchford. In some cases, universities have also served as focal points, as Memorial University has done in Newfoundland. Independents, free from ties to State production, are not required to interpret Canada for Canadians or anyone else, though their films may have to meet the educational needs of TV or the schools, or may be promotional and instructional as corporately sponsored films usually are. Others stake out territory the State agencies do not cover or political ideologies that challenge the general sanction.

The documentaries meant for commercial markets often borrow themes and structures from popular journalism or use ready-made events such as the Griersonian production cycle, the artistic performance that pervades TV, or the portrait of an individual as moral exemplar and prodigious spectacle. The prevailing ideological tendency in such films is the broad, liberal humanism familiar from many NFB works, emphasizing continuities—across age-boundaries, national frontiers, social divisions, and time—but dwelling less on national cultural projects. The Saltzmans' long series of films for television, 'Spread Your Wings', (1975–81) is a good example of a creative cycle used to give structure (usually the production of a crafted object), but here the artisans are scattered across the world and are all children. In his *Cooperage* (1975, CFA) Borsós cut in parallel, tinted archival footage of the barrel-making processes, establishing continuity with a pioneering past, as he did again in his astonishing *Spartree* (1977, CFA), on the exploits of the tree-toppers who prepare spartrees for the high-lead system of log moving in B.C.'s remote and mountainous forests. In Toronto, the most memorable of Rhombus Media's films on musical performances are not those that celebrate virtuoso ability but those that tie music into community, as in **Larry Weinstein**'s *Making Overtures* (1985), an upbeat and cleverly edited portrait of a community orchestra in the small Ontario town of Cobourg that won an Oscar nomination, or that explore continuities between music and nature, as in *Music for Wilderness Lake* (Niv Fichman, Barbara Sweete, and Larry Weinstein, 1980), which captures an original piece of wilderness music—by the experimental composer Murray Schafer—performed on a lake near Bancroft, Ont.

At times Canadian documentary has seemed obsessed with children, often using the classical commonplace of the unexpectedly mature child as an attribute of special status (*puer senex*), but in recent years it has also produced portraits of the unexpectedly youthful old person: **Deepa Saltzman**'s *At 99: A Portrait of Louise Tandy Murch* (1974, **CFA**), which shows the ninety-ninth birthday and daily round of a remarkably active friend of her husband; **Barbara Sweete**'s *Cowboys Don't Cry* (1978–84), in which her octogenarian grandfather relives his cowboy past in Western Canada; and *Don't Mess with Bill* (**Pen Densham & John Watson**, 1980), in which octogenarian Bill Underwood demonstrates his own self-defence system.

Two former students of Sheridan College, near Toronto, **Janis Cole** and **Holly Dale** have explored the margins of society in jointly-made documentaries about body-rub parlours, transvestites, prostitutes, and prison inmates. Their films, often empirical in style, present their subjects without moral judgement or analytical commentary; however, by including details that suggest parallels with the routines and norms of non-deviant behaviour and feelings, they display a passionate humanism. Their explorations of the world of the criminally insane (*Thin Line*, 1977), women in prison (*4W: Prison for Women*, 1981, **CFA**), or Vancouver prostitutes (*Hookers on Davie*, 1984), deliver a body-blow to moral certainties and to notions of clear demarcation lines between deviance and mainstream life.

The moral point of view in the radical feminist films of **Bonnie Kreps**, on the other hand, is unequivocal. *After the Vote* (1969) became the rallying film for the women's movement in the seventies; *This Film Is About Rape* (1978) approached rape through women's reminiscences, dispelling commonly-held myths and telling women what to do about it; *No Life for a Woman* (1979) looked critically at the place assigned to women in company towns.

Films by **Ron Mann** and **Brigitte Berman** document performances and performing artists. Mann's two full-length anthologies, *Imagine the Sound* (1981), showcasing the music of four jazz players, and *Poetry in Motion* (1982), featuring performances by twenty-four Canadian and American poets, have won him many international prizes. Brigitte Berman has made two absorbing feature-length jazz biographies, meticulously researched and illustrated, *Bix, 'Ain't None of Them Play Like Him Yet'* (1982) on trumpeter Bix Beiderbecke, and the Oscar-winning *Artie Shaw: Time Is All You've Got* (1984), which thrives on the clarinettist's compelling personality and story-telling style.

When portrait films and the compilations incorporate material from the film-maker's personal world, distinctions between the documentary and the experimental are blurred, as we have seen in some of the NFB's personal documentaries. Best known among the independents are **Bonnie Kreps**' *Portrait of My Mother* (1973), **Sandy Wilson**'s *Growing Up in Paradise* (1977), and **Barbara Sternberg**'s *The Good Times* (1986).

Although TV documentary is beyond the scope of this book the work of CBC's Vancouver Film Unit in the 1950s must be mentioned, not least because it nurtured the career of **Allan King** (*q.v.* Chapter 5), whose early film there, *Skid Row* (1956), on three Vancouver alcoholics, is often cited as a precursor to Unit B's 'Candid-Eye' series. CBC's series 'Document' (1964–66) was an influential showcase of Canadian documentary: *The Mills of the Gods: Viet Nam* (**Beryl Fox**, 1965) was named Canadian Film of the Year in 1966.

Harry Rasky has specialized in award-winning biographies.

Also on the margins of mainstream documentary is the work done for special events and places. Occasional films have flourished in Canada, especially in the sponsored films made for World Fairs, like Montreal's Expo '67 and Vancouver's Expo '86. Spectacular technical innovations abound: enhanced split-screen, multi-image projection in **Christopher Chapman**'s award-winning *A Place to Stand* (1967) for the Ontario Pavilion; the ultra-bright 60 frames-per-second, 70-mm. Showscan process that appeared in Expo '86 with Donald Brittain's *Terravision* in the Canada Pavilion and Rob Turner's *Discovery* in the B.C. Pavilion; the multi-screen projections pioneered by Czech immigrant **Emil Radok** for the Czech Pavilion in Expo '67 and fully developed in the extraordinary montage effects of his *Taming of the Demons* for the Canada Pavilion in Vancouver. Most impressive of all has been the IMAX process developed by Graeme Ferguson's Multi-Screen Corporation in Cambridge, Ont., with Roman Kroitor and Robert Kerr. With new 70-mm. technology for both camera and projector, films are projected on a six-storey screen inside theatres specially built for the purpose, such as Toronto's Cinesphere at Ontario Place. The most satisfying films are those showing natural scenes like Ferguson's own *North of Superior* (1971) and Chapman's *Volcano* (1973). By adding a specially made fish-eye lens, Omnimax was created to permit dome projection, first featured in 1973 at San Diego's 'Space Theatre'. More recently 3-D Imax has come to crown the heightened realism of the other processes in Chapman's 1984 film for the Science North theatre in Sudbury, Ont., and in the spectacular feature-length *Transitions* (Colin Low & Tony Ianzelo, 1986) for Vancouver's Canada Pavilion again. The films recall the spirit of the first films by the Lumière brothers that attracted their public, too, with illusions of natural space, forms, and movement.

3

DOCUMENTARY FILM IN FRENCH SINCE 1939

THE FIRST FRENCH-CANADIAN WAVE AT THE NFB 1941–51

The process of developing French-language film-making at the NFB was laborious and slow. The Canadian Government Motion Picture Bureau employed no French Canadians, nor were any on staff at Montreal's Associated Screen News (despite Sparling's pæan to the bilingual city in *Rhapsody in Two Languages* , 1934). Film-making in Quebec had been limited to travelling churchmen and, in the absence of any broader tradition, French-language films were a low priority when the NFB began. But they were soon needed to promote the war effort. The first pieces in French released by the NFB were short news items on Quebec military training camps. In 1940–41 a few French-language films were contracted out to Gerald Noxon at ASN and to Budge and Judith Crawley, best known of which is *Un du 22e* (Noxon, 1941), a fictional short promoting enlistment.

It was December 1941 when the first francophone film-maker, **Vincent Paquette**, came to the Board. From a small production office in Montreal, he directed the NFB's first in-house French-language production, *La cité de Notre-Dame* (1942), a thirty-minute colour film for Montreal's Tercentenary, made with Budge and Judith Crawley and a young composer called Maurice Blackburn. Within a year, Paquette was in Ottawa heading a small group of French Canadians editing stock shots and 'versioning': making French-language versions of the theatrical wartime series. From 1943 they produced a French news magazine from 'versioned' material and locally-shot items on Quebec. By 1945 the French-Canadian staff had grown to seventeen, and the bilingual **Guy Glover** was the producer of a French Language Program. But the French Canadians were thinly spread across a number of series and programs and lacked the homogeneity and collective spirit that characterized the late fifties and sixties.

From the wartime group, **Jean Palardy** made traditional NFB documentaries about regional arts and crafts—such as *Le vent qui chante* / *Music in the Wind* (CCO, 1945) on the Casavant pipe organs of Saint-Hyacinthe, and *Peintres populaires de Charlevoix* / *Primitive Painters of Charlevoix* ('Canadian Artists', 1946)—and the co-operative movement, best represented by *Marée montante* / *The Rising Tide* (1949), on the Antigonish movement of the Maritimes in the thirties, a film that combined the usual voice of authority and that of a fictitious Cape Breton fisherman over documentary footage and dramatic sequences. **Pierre Pétel**'s short documentaries were characterized by a slower reflective rhythm, and a more personal style in the commentary when it was used. With Maurice Blackburn's musical score, *Terre de Caïn* ('Vigie' series, 1949), about life on the North Shore (the 'land God gave to Cain'), was the first French-language documentary to win a CFA. **Maurice Blackburn** later made his reputation with experimental sound-tracks for Norman McLaren's animated films, and his music has been featured in many landmark films in Quebec.

By 1950 the French-Canadian group had grown to include Roger Blais, Raymond Garceau, Victor Jobin, Bernard Devlin and Jacques Bobet—men who provided the base of production experience for the Quebec Golden Age of the sixties. But the early years were hard going. In the late forties only a quarter of the NFB budget went to French-language production; indeed, if French versioning is discounted, the proportion was closer to an eighth. Often the only route to experience lay with English units. **Raymond Garceau**, who studied agriculture at Ste-Anne-de-la-Pocatière, joined Lawrence Cherry's Agricultural Unit filming, as he says, 'in every pigpen, cowshed and chicken coop from Halifax to Vancouver' ('with tripods caked in muck and cables coated in slime, it was direct cinema for sure !').

Pressure for improved French-language production came from the Massey Commission (1951) and Quebec playwright Gratien Gélinas, a new member of the NFB's Board of Governors. In 1949 the NFB had released seventy original films in English, but only four in French.

Of course, Premier Duplessis did not help the cause in Quebec. His distaste for the NFB had led to sweeping restrictions on film circulation in the province.

TELEVISION AND THE GROWTH OF FRENCH-LANGUAGE PRODUCTION 1952–64

The coming of French-language television in 1952 was a timely stimulant for NFB production in French. **Bernard Devlin** and **Roger Blais**, who had taken over the senior production role for French-language films from Guy Glover, did not agree on the appropriate direction to follow. Blais was for cultural entertainment programming, adaptations of literary works by Canadian authors, and a showcase for the performing arts—typified by his five-part 1953 'Horizons' series. But Devlin's TV reportage won the argument. Not only was it cheaper, but the use of pre-recorded voice-over, music, and sound effects kept post-production to a minimum and meant the Board had full control of production before shooting began. Devlin's approach, first used in the English 'On the Spot' in 1953, was soon paralleled by the 26-part French series 'Sur le Vif', using original material and hosted by Gil Laroche. But the series' emphasis on safe magazine journalism about prominent institutions (the army, the police, the church, the Better Business Bureau) left no room for critical probing. Although Devlin's approach anticipated later *cinéma direct* shooting methods, there were also marked differences. *Cinéma direct* film-makers adopted a more improvisational shooting style with minimal script and an offsetting emphasis on editing, an approach that avoided pre-production control.

'Passe-Partout' (1955–57), the successor to 'Sur le vif', was a more ambitious undertaking: fifty-two programs including French originals and versions of films in the 'Perspective' series. Dramatized episodes and case-histories of all kinds accompanied compilations of archival footage and traditional voice-over documentary. Social themes dominated but the series lacked any common perspective. Its importance lay in the start it gave to newcomers, such as Louis Portugais, Léonard Forest, Fernand Dansereau, Claude Jutra, and Pierre Patry.

All in all, it could be argued that by 1958 things were looking good for French film-making. Federally licensed television had provided an outlet for films otherwise hampered by the exhibition constraints imposed by a hostile Quebec government. In 1954 the francophone **Pierre Juneau** left French-language film distribution to become the Commissioner's special assistant for francophone affairs and gradually accumulated executive authority over French production. After years of delay, the Board's headquarters were moved to Montreal in 1956, at more than arm's length from government and in an environment more congenial to the francophones. One year later the NFB acquired its first French-Canadian Commissioner, **Guy Roberge**, the youngest Commissioner since Grierson himself and one of the most active. In two years (1956–57) the Board succeeded in attracting many French Canadians: Claude Jutra, Michel Brault, Fernand Dansereau, Gilles Groulx, Clément Perron, Michel Régnier, Jean Dansereau, Claude Fournier, Pierre Patry, Marcel Carrière, Georges Dufaux, Bernard Gosselin. By 1964 they had been joined by Jacques Godbout, Gilles Carle, Arthur Lamothe, Pierre Perrault, Jean Beaudin, Anne-Claire Poirier, Jean-Claude Labrecque, and Michel Moreau.

This young generation of Quebec film-makers was compared by many with the contemporary New Wave of film-makers in France. The social and political climate certainly favoured their success. Duplessis died in 1959 and a year later Jean Lesage's Liberals won the Quebec election on a platform of social reform and modernization that would sweep away the parochialism and clericalism of the old Quebec. In 1963 Lester Pearson's Liberals were returned to power in Ottawa and would soon commit themselves to a national policy of bilingualism and biculturalism. In this context the summit of franco-phone film-makers' aspirations seemed to be realized in 1964 when the NFB established a French-language Production Branch— with its own Director of Production (Pierre Juneau) and freedom from the influence and priorities of English-language film production.

However, all was not plain sailing from 1952 to a happy ending in 1964. Internal dissension over the place of drama at the NFB in the fifties was matched by intense debate over feature film production in the sixties. Power struggles in the late 1950s were exacerbated by dismay over the low proportion of French-language originals—out-numbered four to one in the Board's figures, almost twenty to one in one report in *Le Devoir*. This disappointment, coupled with a strong feeling that senior executives were discriminating against French-Canadian employees when Roger Blais was forced out in 1957, led to a virulent French campaign against the NFB in *Le Devoir* and the French-language nationalist press. Although the new directors soon won international recognition, many fell afoul of the 'general sanction' and cries of censorship and political interference were heard again. In 1964, at the height of the ferment, five of the NFB's francophone directors (Godbout, Carle, Perron, Arcand, and Groulx) contributed to a special number of the left-wing journal *parti pris*, denouncing the Board for its limits on freedom of expression, its refusal to embark on feature film production, and its colonial role in Quebec. Pierre Juneau reprimanded the 'offenders' and insisted on scaling down the 'personal' flavour of future French-language documentaries. Demotions followed and an exodus of some of the NFB's finest talent, among them Carle, Brault, Lamothe, Gosselin, and Groulx. In 1966 Jacques Bobet, one of those to suffer demotion, wrote bitterly in *Liberté*:

> In fifteen months the counter-revolution destroyed the work of fifteen years: the finest group of film-makers ever brought together in Canada was decimated, scattered, dropped into a void with vague promises, never kept, of aid to film production. And so we wasted the most original cultural resource this country had ever had.

THE GOLDEN AGE OF QUEBEC DOCUMENTARY 1957–64

The French-language documentary films made while Guy Roberge was Commissioner have been given special status in Canadian film history. Although many of the films appeared in the television series 'Temps présent', they quickly secured extensive theatrical and non-theatrical distribution. They were featured in special numbers of film magazines in France and began drawing prizes at international festivals.

Two profound changes had intersected: the social and political change in Quebec, and the technical, economic, and aesthetic change in the world of film. The Quiet Revolution was in many ways reflected in the young urban intellectuals now turning their cameras towards Quebec. University-educated, including poets, journalists, and novelists, they believed in the need for social change and many would support the independence movement. In addition, they were avid enthusiasts of film: they were active in the students' ciné-club movement from the fifties; some wrote for the new film journals; and Jutra and Brault, who had already won a CFA with an amateur film, collaborated on a thirteen-part series of programs about the cinema for Radio-Canada ('Images en boîte' 1954–5).

The group embraced two apparently contradictory positions. They endorsed the idea of the uncontrolled documentary, rejecting detailed shooting-scripts and the staging of pro-filmic action. At the same time, they favoured the cultivation of a personal vision, with the elevation of the director to the status of *auteur*. If the improvisational style is clearly central to the empirical style of the Candid-Eye, the idea of the personal vision derives more from the French critics of the influential *Cahiers du Cinéma*. But in Quebec, the film-makers also had a sense of a collective mission. **Gilles Carle**, looking back on those times, identified this mission as the expression of solidarity with the society they were filming: 'Our films were above all an impassioned appropriation of the social milieu. The picturesque (the outsider's view) has yielded to the familiar; the myth has yielded in the face of reality.' The cameraman **Michel Brault** expressed the change technically as the wide-angle style. This consisted 'simply in approaching the people and filming them, *participating in their lives* and not observing them in secret, inside a box, or from high up in a window with a tele-photo lens' (my emphasis).

The landmark was *Les Raquetteurs* (1958). An unprepared filmgoer watching it now may be puzzled by the importance of this 15-minute portrait of events at a snowshoe festival in Sherbrooke. And yet it typified the approach, the technique, and the spirit of the Quebec Golden Age. *Les Raquetteurs* brought together a cameraman (Michel Brault), an editor (Gilles Groulx) and, in a minor role, a sound technician (Marcel Carrière), none of whom assumed the role of director. It was expanded from its original purpose (a four-minute TV clip) without prior permission, and when Grant McLean consigned the rushes to stock-shots back at head office it was finished secretly by Groulx. The film won support from Unit B's Tom Daly and others, and gained release. It went on to be featured at the Flaherty Symposium in California, to win a Silver Plaque in an Italian Festival, and to enter the canon of the new documentary.

The film's first shot affirms the new style, taken amidst the street revellers without traditional establishing shots. Using hand-held 35-mm cameras, it showed with minimal explanation various incidents in a small-town festival. Moments of wry humour or knockdown fun led some English critics to view the film as mockingly satirical, but the film was rarely seen in this light in Quebec, where the treatment was considered sympathetic. The film did not adopt the distant, ironic smile of the 'Candid Eye' films or the commentaries of Donald Brittain. Instead, it declared solidarity with the people it was watching and returned this image to them. This new style might have been new to the NFB, but it was not new in Quebec film-making (see Chapters 1 and 4).

What *was* new to Quebec was the focus on urban rituals rather than rural round. This would dominate French Unit films for the next six years: ritualized violence in body-contact sports (boxing in *Golden Gloves*, Groulx, 1961; wrestling in *La Lutte*, collective, 1961; hockey in *Un jeu si simple*, Groulx, 1963), the Montrealers' ritual of the wintertime Florida vacation (*Voir Miami*, Groulx, 1962); or the arrival of American tourists in summertime Quebec City (*Québec USA*, Jutra & Brault, 1962). The films frequently incorporated scenes from city dance-floors or children's street games. Ritual implies rhythm, cycle, and performance. By employing camera movements and editing patterns that replicated the rhythms they found, the self-conscious film-makers of the French Unit tied their film-making into the celebration. Whether shot in the direct style or not, the films were often edited to coincide with a cycle shown in the film. They often open with arrivals and close with departures, as in *Jour après jour* (Perron, 1962), on life in a small paper-mill town, or *Les Bûcherons de la Manouane*, Lamothe, 1962), on life in the logging camps. The natural time-cycle of the day constantly brackets the film, as in the waking-day of *A Saint-Henri le cinq septembre* (Hubert Aquin *et al.*, 1962) or the twenty-four hours of *Les bacheliers de la cinquième* (Perron, 1962). Such time-cycles occurred in the old Proulx and Tessier films celebrating the natural life; however, by signalling the end of a day with the Montreal Forum's dimming lights (*Un jeu si simple*), Groulx chose an unabashed urban alternative to the lakeside sunset. Rituals also contain elements of performance for a public. The Quebec film-makers did not exclude the watching public, but frequently showed it in their films. They often present the picture of a collective engaged in watching a formalized projection of itself. Destined to return an image of the familiar to that same public, they could be construed as an extension of that process. By echoing the rhythms of the ritual, by adopting similarly cyclical structures, and by endorsing watching as an essential constituent part of its celebration, the films expressed their solidarity with the new Quebec.

Not all the films were as uncritical as this analysis might suggest. Some of the rhetorical devices mentioned above were harnessed to ends other than building ethnic self-assurance. Clément Perron's *Les bacheliers de la cinquième* and *Jour après jour* presented views of alienated youth and the alienating workplace respectively. These films are scripted, although the inclusion of songs and the prosodic rhythms of the voice-over soften their expository impact. Their montage sequences show that the Griersonian tradition was intact. One editing device in *Les bacheliers de la cinquième* illustrates the solidarity effect. The film opens and closes with a series of dreamy pans over the riverscape of the North Shore; but whereas the opening sequence shows them uncut as traditional exposition, the closing sequence shows them intercut with the gazing face of an unemployed youth who has just slept out on the river bank and whose vain attempts to find a job have been the subject of the film. The peaceful landscape, seen through the eyes of the boy, is now a barren workplace. The film-maker has come to share his protagonist's view and makes that sharing visible to the spectator. Lamothe's *Les Bûcherons de la Manouane* also used rhythmic visual editing and sound montage to emphasize the way the logger's work in amassing the resources demanded by the urban market has been mechanized. But such films, and others by Gilles Groulx, soon fell afoul of the NFB's 'general sanction'. Phrases or references thought to be critical of the prevailing social order were removed. In *Normétal* (Groulx, 1959) scenes of the mine were intercut with scenes of everyday life beyond it to connote the enslaving character of the workplace—dominating and engulfing every aspect of the workers' lives. Considered too critical, the film was re-cut and halved, with the result that Groulx refused to let his name stand in the credits.

While some film-makers chafed at the bit of institutional conservatism, others, like Gilles Carle and Jacques Godbout, were beginning to feel that the direct style was too limiting and superficial to satisfy their authorial aspirations. **Gilles Carle** even made a film called *Solange dans nos campagnes* (1964) that sent up the direct cinema style: it showed a trip to the country to film a slice of farm life and interview a country girl that failed to reveal anything about farm life or its problems. Shortly after this came the exodus into the private sector. Many of the team formed private companies, or went into freelance work or television.

CINÉMA DIRECT AND THE FEATURE DOCUMENTARY

The spirit of the *cinéma direct* did not die. It continued most notably in projects where the film-makers lived with their subjects over extended periods and edited the mountains of film they shot into feature films or cycles of features. Several Quebec film-makers followed this direction.

Guy L. Côté, from the fifties' generation and with much experience in English-language production, returned to French-language documentary with a diptych of collectively-signed direct features on the state of the Catholic Church called *Tranquillement pas vite* (1972). The first part, which documented—in a series of montage-sequences—discussions about the collapse of the traditional Church, was structured around the striking, Buñuelesque images of the demolition of Montreal's Ste-Cunégonde church; the second part attempted to demonstrate, in diary form, a new kind of religious practice—the socially engaged base community of which Côté was a member. The two films constitute two versions of direct cinema: the interlocking of discussions with dream-like, symbolic scenes; and the uncommentated chronology of the life of a closely-knit group of people.

Georges Dufaux, another veteran from the late fifties who had worked on the 'Candid-Eye' series, produced a number of features that made use of his Unit B experience and raised questions about social policy in Quebec. A study of life in an emergency ward focused attention on hospitals and health care (*A votre santé*, 1973); the difficult transition to institutional care for the aged through the experience of one elderly couple being separated (*Au bout de mon âge* / *At the end of my Days*, 1975); and life for the elderly in residential settings (*Les jardins d'hiver*, 1976). Then Dufaux turned his attention to the school system with the eight-part 'Les enfants des normes' (1979). Five years later he brought back many of the students in the feature *Les enfants des normes—POST-SCRIPTUM* , (1983). *L'espace d'un été* (André Melançon, 1980) was another project that involved interaction with children. **André Melançon** accompanied, without prompting, three 12-year-olds during their summer holidays in Montreal. But Côté, Dufaux, and Melançon are not the prime representatives of the direct feature. That role is reserved for Pierre Perrault.

The reputation of **Pierre Perrault** does not rest solely on his films. He is also a poet, a dramatist, and an essayist. But his films on Quebec's history and heartland now dominate the picture we have of him today. It was during his radio broadcasts on Quebec's lower St Lawrence in 1956 that he found himself drawn into the spoken testimony of local people, when he realized that 'what the miller was saying about the sound of his millwheel turning had more beauty than the sound of the millwheel itself'. From then on the spoken word became for him the true local heritage, uncontrolled by distant élites, unmediated by foreign technologies, uncalcified by transcription into written form. And as he recorded the spoken testimony of the Tremblay family on the Ile-aux-Coudres Perrault found the key to his own sense of cultural identity.

Soon Perrault had a chance to turn his radio series into film, and 1959 saw him embarked on a Radio-Canada series by Crawley Films. Under René Bonnière's direction, Perrault wrote the script for thirteen films with the series title *Au Pays de Neufve France* / *St. Lawrence North*. Working on his first shoot, Perrault soon realized the gulf that separated him from the traditional Bonnière. He tells how, when shooting the scene where some islanders are digging a boat out of a snow-bank, Bonnière prevented an unscheduled passer-by from entering the shot to help out. For Bonnière this was done to protect the shot, as the camera was meant to record it; but for Perrault it constituted an unpardonable intrusion into the natural order of island behaviour. Thenceforth, his rule was, 'Never prevent the things being filmed from taking their course'.

Perrault subsequently joined the NFB, where he has remained to this day. During his years there he has completed cycles of films on life in L'Ile aux Coudres, the Abitibi farming communities in northwest Quebec, and life among the Montagnais peoples of the Subarctic; a document of a francophone students' protest at Moncton university; a lengthy, more analytical compilation on the nature of nationalism; and studies of a hunting weekend near Maniwaki, a trip to Saint-Malo in search of Jacques Cartier, and the voyage from Saint-Malo to the Gulf of Saint Lawrence.

The strong nationalist overtones in his work, especially *Un pays sans bon sens* (1970), strained the 'general sanction' at the NFB and led to restricted circulation for a time. Of fourteen features, only five are available in English versions—four using the regrettable method of superimposing English commentaries over dimly heard French— and two lost more than thirty minutes in the transfer.

In the Ile-aux-Coudres cycle, *Pour la suite du monde* (1963) showed the islanders collectively reviving a traditional form of beluga-hunt in the St Lawrence. *Le règne du jour* (1966) accompanied the Tremblays to France in a search for their French roots. *Voitures d'eau* (1968) described the dying years of the locally-built water-schooners that used to ply the river. From life around the Tremblay family, the village raconteur Louis Harvey, and the boatmen of the island—who all achieved a kind of stardom from these works in Quebec—Perrault moved to the Abitibi region, where one of Quebec's biggest dramas had been played out over four decades. Abitibi had been opened up and settled when the Quebec establishment decided that agricultural development provided the solution to a city-driven depression. *Un royaume vous attend* (1975), *Le retour à la terre* (1976), and *Gens d'Abitibi* (1979) reveal the subsequent depopulation of the northern farms and focus on Hauris Lalancette, a local farmer fighting to preserve their way of life. As houses are trucked away along the highways, we see hulks of abandoned farmsteads; we meet the octogenarian Cyrille Labrecque, still clearing land after forty years at it; and we learn that the land laboriously cleared over thirty years by one settler was sold and replanted with trees in eleven days flat. Perrault gives ironic evidence of the rhetoric that sustained the early dream by intercutting Proulx's films into *Le retour à la terre* . In the last film the onset of northern development and the St James Bay highway complete the cycle of depopulation and wage-dependence. The cycle includes another trip to France—this time Lalancette's—with parallels of regional neglect and decline (*C'était un Québécois en Bretagne, Madame !*, 1977).

In his recent films Perrault seems more of an outsider to the communities he visits. The trips to the Montagnais peoples' land in the Subarctic consist of a complex of intercut journeys by whites that serve both as a catalyst to the Indians' talk of the threat of sedentary existence and assimilation, and as a locus for opposition between the whites who want to help the Indians and the anti-interventionists who try to avoid colonial paternalism but feel powerless against greater historical forces.

Although Perrault never appears on screen, the films often include characters who seem to have an affinity with the film-maker. In *Un pays sans bon sens* the geneticist Didier Dufour, returning to his native Baie St-Paul, gives a speech on the continuity between parochial attachments to birthplace and the sense of belonging to a greater community that rehearses Perrault's own beliefs. In *La bête lumineuse* (1982) and *Les voiles bas et en travers* (1983) the enquiry about the meaning of the subject of the film—the hunting trip ritual or the place of Jacques Cartier in Saint-Malo—is carried by the young poet, Stéphane-Albert Boulais. His desire to explore through the creative word acts as Perrault's foil for the raw self-assurance of the characters whose experience he tries to share.

Perrault catches the ritualized processes of collective self-affirmation, through forms of cultural expression—the spoken word, the craftsman's gesture, the tribal ceremony that resist mediation by distant authorities. It can be argued that preserving such a record is at odds with the way of life being celebrated: the impulses of the living word, the reflections of the living gesture are registered in an inert material controlled by a distant authority (a federal institution no less). The riposte lies in the active role Perrault ascribes to the film's audience. As he says: 'this is not a transparent kind of cinema . . . a new form of reading must be devised for this new kind of cinema . . . the film is realized in the theatre.' In this sense Perrault's *cinéma direct* can be an alternative, experimental kind of film practice.

Before leaving *cinéma direct*, we should recall an important alternative to the projects of Perrault and others, the work of **Michel Moreau**, for many years with the NFB and the Office du Film du Québec, but since 1973 running his own production company Éducfilm. Moreau's psycho-social *mises en situations*, in which he researched with his subjects important moments in their lives and re-staged them with the subject playing out the central role, offer an approach particularly suited to the more traumatic experiences that Moreau wants us to share with society's rejects, primarily the handicapped, the disabled, the mentally retarded, and the terminally ill. His best work is in the features *La leçon des mongoliens* (1974), *Jules le magnifique* (1976), and *Les traces d'un homme* (1981), as well as his upbeat critique of lotteries in *Le Million tout-puissant* (1985), which dwelt on the experiences of winners.

THE ACTIVIST FILM IN QUEBEC

There were other film-makers at the same time for whom a realignment of the relationship between audience and film meant social commitment. The French Production Branch established 'Société Nouvelle' in tandem with the 1968 'Challenge for Change' program, although they had already been experimenting with this kind of film in Fernand Dansereau's Groupe de Recherches Sociales. **Raymond Garceau** had already made a 26-film series on rural planning and agricultural development, the 'ARDA' films (1965–66), which used film as a communicative tool in community planning for change. **Michel Régnier** had shot *L'Ecole des autres* (1968), a film that followed the setting up and the course of PASS, a project undertaken by a group of education activists, to tackle the problems of Inner City schools and students. **Fernand Dansereau** himself had made *Saint-Jérôme* (1968), a film on the impact of technological change on a small town that showed and stimulated processes for community involvement in social reconstruction. **Maurice Bulbulian**'s *La p'tite Bourgogne* (1968) showed how film could be used in a citizens' battle against urban renewal in Montreal.

As the Société Nouvelle program got under way, some works did maintain the goal of making film and video technology available to a community to pursue its own course as Bonnie Klein had done in the Montreal's *Saint-Jacques*. In *La noce est pas finie* (1971) **Léonard Forest** showed a group of New Brunswick Acadians coming together to discuss, script, and act out a film. More often the film-makers retained their control of the medium to give voice to various forms of social dissent. Thus Bulbulian's *Dans nos forêts* (1971) documented unrest among workers in the forest industry, and his *Richesse des autres* (1973) accompanied a group of Abitibi miners on a visit to the newly nationalized mines in Salvador Allende's Chile. Best known of all these works are Michel Régnier's fifteen-film series 'Urbanose'

(1972) on urban planning and development and the need for citizen participation, and 'Urba 2000' (1974), which examined various options and solutions in different parts of the world. The Griersonian division into problem and solution on a grand scale can be traced back to Legg's 1939 film on youth unemployment.

More recently, **Jean Chabot**'s *La fiction nucléaire* (1978) has continued the tradition of the Quebec social documentary by entering the nuclear energy debate. **Fernand Bélanger**'s *De la tourbe et du restant* (1979), ostensibly a documentary about the peat-industry, uses the peat to symbolize the principles of exploitation and domination—man over nature, man over man, and one national culture over another. Similarly, **Robert Favreau**'s *Le soleil a pas d'chance* (1975), at first sight a documentary on the world of Quebec's Carnival Queens, stands as a condemnation of the exploitation of women in a sexist consumer society. Finally, **Diane Létourneau**'s privately made feature *Les servantes du bon Dieu* (1978), a gentle documentary portrait of life in a Sherbrooke community of nuns, subtly reveals without comment the subservience of the women to the male hierarchy of the Church.

Outside the NFB the activist film was exemplified in the work of both **Arthur Lamothe** and the Marxist CIP-Champ Libre group. In 1965 Lamothe left the NFB to found the Société générale cinématographique. *Le mépris n'aura qu'un temps* (1970) is his major work to emerge from that company. Under union sponsorship, it explored the Montreal construction industry, giving voice to workers' grievances, to concern over industrial accidents, and to nascent class-consciousness. In 1972 Lamothe founded Les Ateliers audio-visuels du Québec, where he made a lengthy series on the Montagnais Indians: 'Chronique des Indiens du Nord-Est du Québec'; the series consists of the eight-part 'Carcajou et le péril blanc' (1974–76) and the four-part 'La terre de l'homme' (1980). Yielding to the grievances and testimony of the Indians themselves in these films, he revealed to the Québécois—at the height of their aspirations to a just redress of their own historic grievances—the fate of the Indians whose land, language, culture, and heritage had been, and were being, irrevocably destroyed by white Europeans of French as well as of English extraction. Made with anthropologist Rémi Savard, these films gave voice to Indian experience and make Perrault's films seem coy or distant by comparison. But if Lamothe's films disclose Indians' grievances in a more confrontational setting, and imply a tougher social analysis than Perrault's, his curious, almost surrealist juxtapositions within the frame, his symphonic editing style, and a tragic sense of destiny reveal common roots within a Québécois tradition.

In 1973 the Comité d'information politique, a film distribution house, and the team from *Champ Libre*, a left-wing film journal launched in 1971, collaborated on a collective film about workers' experience of class struggle over a two-year period. The film was *On a raison de se révolter* (1973), and although some members of the group thought it was guilty of wishful thinking about the level of class consciousness it set out to portray, it is an example of a kind of film-making impossible in the NFB.

Three films ran afoul of NFB censorship during the fateful decade following the CEGEP sit-ins of 1968, a period dominated by Sidney Newman's Commissionership. Jacques Leduc's *Cap d'espoir* (1969) was more of a political satire than a documentary, written in a style that recalls the Yippies and the spirit of May '68 in France. Denys Arcand's *On est au coton* (1970) was a lengthy exposé of life in the textile industry, particularly of the workers' grievances. By using the direct style and allowing the sound-track to bear prolonged witness to the inhumanly noisy conditions of work, the film made a persuasive case about workers' alienation, though it offered little hope for change. Gilles Groulx's *24 heures ou plus* (1972) did offer hopes for radical social change: a careful montage of the evidence of news clips gathered from the public information media over a two-month period was accompanied by the film-maker's own forthright commentary. All three films were eventually 'liberated' by Newman's successor, André Lamy, in 1977, although *Cap d'espoir* is no longer listed in the current NFB French catalogue.

THE FEMINIST TRANSFORMATION OF THE ACTIVIST FILM

The first organized steps towards a women's cinema in Quebec came from the Société Nouvelle program with the series 'En Tant que Femmes' (1973–74) produced by Anne-Claire Poirier. The films, usually an hour each, concentrated on the experience of womanhood in contemporary Quebec, using either scripted docudramas or direct documentary techniques. Most of those involved in the films, including all directors and scriptwriters, were women. The films of the early seventies raised questions about child care and daycare (*A qui appartient ce gage ?*, collective, 1973); cast a critical eye over the historical role of women in Quebec (*Les filles du roy / They called us 'Les Filles du Roy'*, Poirier, 1974); and frankly discussed the need for new roles for women growing up (*Les filles c'est pas pareil*, Hélène Girard, 1974), in their relations with men (*J'me marie, j'me marie pas*, Mireille Dansereau, 1973), and as wives and mothers (*Souris, tu m'inquiètes* , Aimée Danis, 1973). They combined fictional and documentary sequences illustrating the source of grievance and the need for change, they showed groups of women in discussions instead of assigning the analysis to a single voice of authority, and they served as stimuli for discussion in the community.

Anne-Claire Poirier was the dominant force behind the emergence of a women's cinema at the Board. She had joined the NFB's French Unit at the peak of its success in 1960 and worked on films directed by Jutra, Groulx, Perron, and Claude Fournier. Although the first woman to direct a feature film in Quebec (*De mère en fille / Mother-to-Be*, 1967), she languished in obscurity at the NFB. In six books published on French-Canadian film-making from 1966 to 1972, neither she nor her work is mentioned once. It took the preparations for International Women's Year in 1975 to win her recognition, and an opportunity to make more features.

Her films consistently defy simple classification. They incorporate fictional, empirical, and personal elements in various ways. This slippage between modes of address to the spectator has often been identified with women's film and indeed throughout her career she has consistently sought to identify her projects with feminist aspirations. Her films deal with issues that put women in a specific social and political context: questions about identity and social role that come with pregnancy and motherhood (*De mère en fille / Mother-to-Be*, 1967); doubts and tensions arising from unwanted pregnancy (*Le temps de l'avant / Before the Time Comes*, 1975); the experience and meaning of rape (*Mourir à tue-tête / A Scream from Silence*, 1979). However, Poirier infuses her films with a strong sense of the personal experience that underlies the broader issue. In *De mère en fille*, she combines a personal diary of her own pregnancy with the actual experience of Liette Desjardins; in *Mourir à tue-tête*, the rape scene is shot to accentuate the victim's personal sense of its duration. Besides showing participants discussing their feelings and principles, the films project issues on to broader political planes: in *De mère en fille* Czech day-care centres are visited; in *Mourir à tue-tête* violation of women is seen through news footage from Europe, Africa, and Vietnam. In *La quarantaine* (1982), Poirier has found another way to intertwine presentation and representation. She brought together a group of ten friends after thirty years apart; their reminiscences, shot as dramatic sequences with other actors, highlight the importance of adolescence and the image we hold of it in middle age as part of the social and personal construction of adult identity. In Poirier's films questions of body personal and body politic are often juxtaposed. In keeping with much feminist theory and practice, she injects her own experiences and views as exemplars of the process of fusing the personal and the collective.

Beyond the NFB, the mixture of genres recurs in *Le grand remue-ménage* (**Sylvie Groulx & Francine Allaire**, 1978), a ferocious, sardonic attack by two young feminist activists on male chauvinism, again intercutting dramatic scenes and two prolonged interviews with cases in point. The interplay of drama and record is quite differently realized in **Jacqueline Levitin**'s *Pas fou comme on le pense* (1985): it shows a group of former psychiatric patients engaged in a communal alternative to traditional, institutional treatment, whose discussions at a weekend session in a country house are interspersed with their own dramatic re-enactments of their experience of madness and psychiatric care. **Sophie Bissonnette** has made more militant social documentaries on working-class women: the award-winning *Une histoire de femmes / A Wives' Tale* (with Joyce Rock and Martin Duckworth, 1980), made co-operatively with the wives of the 1978 INCO strikers in Sudbury, Ont., and *Quel numéro / What Number?: The Electronic Workshop* (1985), which dealt with the computerization of work primarily done by women. **Joseé Beaudet**'s *Le Film d'Ariane* (1985) is a meticulously assembled compilation history of women in Quebec from 1925 to the present.

CELEBRATIONS OF PERFORMANCE AND HERITAGE

The recent trend towards films intended to preserve ethno-cultural heritage and performance was not universally welcomed. Bernard-

Richard Emond's 1980 attack recalls Grierson's denunciation of the CGMPB's films of the thirties: 'a foreign spectator randomly viewing a dozen documentaries of recent vintage would probably get the impression that Quebec is a rural, traditional society and that Quebeckers spend their time dancing jigs, singing along, ploughing fields and weaving arrow sashes'. Others, such as Pierre Véronneau or Pierre Demers, greeted the trend as a celebration of popular culture proclaiming the new national consciousness.

The new ethnographic film can be traced to **Léo Plamondon** in Trois Rivières. His films document, often in close-up, the manual skills of artisans at work making violins, at the forge, in the harness-shop, or fishing for eels, with the words of the craftsman as voice-over. Best known is his collaboration with Bernard Gosselin on *La belle ouvrage* (1977–80), a 21-film series co-produced by the NFB and Radio-Canada. Many ethnographic film-makers are cameramen, who had worked on cycles like those of Pierre Perrault, and who bear witness through their choice of shots, angles, movements and framing devices, as in **Bernard Gosselin**'s *César et son canot d'écorce / César's Bark-Canoe* (1971) in which César Newashish, an Indian from the Manowan reserve, engages in every successive stage of building the canoe from the collection of the natural materials to the launching, and draws us not only into a craft but also into a way of living in nature. In the feature film *Jean Carignan, Violoneux* (1975), Gosselin provided the musical portrait of the doyen of fiddlers and became so interested in the Gallo-Celtic tradition of fiddling that he went on to make *La veillée des veillées* (1976). In a collective marathon recalling the heyday of the NFB's French Units, Gosselin assembled the finest cinematographers and sound engineers. They shot and recorded André Gladu's concert that brought together traditional musicians from Quebec, Louisiana, Acadia, Ireland, and Brittany. Performance, celebration, and collective affirmation of common roots combined to give this film the mystique of ritual. Shortly thereafter **Michel Brault** made 'Le Son des Français d'Amérique' (1976–77), a 15-film series with André Gladu on the traditional music of French communities throughout America. NFB's Acadian Studio produced *Le frolic cé pour ayder* (Laurent Comeau, *et al.*, 1979), on one of the annual Acadian music festivals at Cap Pelé N.B. that celebrate the tradition of the 'frolic' (Acadian for bee or barn-raising).

Finally, in the context of the celebration of collective performance, the documentary films of Jean-Claude Labrecque and Roger Frappier elevate observations of various forms of performance into collective rituals in the Golden Age style. **Jean-Claude Labrecque**'s *60 cycles* (1965), a lyrical observational film of the Tour du Saint-Laurent, has won more international awards for the NFB—thirteen—than any other Quebec documentary. A decade later Labrecque was the natural choice to head the team making *The Games of the XXI Olympiad* , the official NFB film of the 1976 Montreal Olympics. Labrecque's *La visite du général de Gaulle au Québec* (1967) treated that fateful visit less as a political event for analysis than as a performance in stages that increasingly engaged the attention of a society in search of occasions for collective celebration, a treatment quite distinct from the ironic detachment of the more journalistic *Du général au particulier* (1967), Claude Fournier's less reverent version of the same occasion. Spectacle was also recorded with emphasis on the spoken word in two poetry marathons financed and staged by the NFB, *La nuit de la poésie (27 mars 1970)* and *La nuit de la poésie 28 mars 1980* . Oddly enough, Labrecque (with Jean-Pierre Masse) chose to concentrate more on the performance than its reception (no audience shots are shown). But the sense of recital and ritual build to a climax of collective affirmation in a dramatically edited film.

After two documentary reportages on Quebec poets for the Office du Film du Québec, **Roger Frappier** lived and shot film in the *cinéma direct* style with an experimental theatre troupe called Le Grand Cirque Ordinaire, interposing scenes from their tour show 'T'es pas tannée Jeanne d'Arc' and conversations with the troupe's members about their place as performers in the changing society of Quebec. This became *Le grand film ordinaire* (1970). He followed this with *L'Infonie inachevée* (1972), another interlace of performances and scenes from the daily life of the experimental group of composers, poets, and painters called l'Infonie.

The heritage of more recent immigrants has been documented and celebrated recently in French-language films by such directors as **Paul Tana** and **Tahani Rached** at the Montreal Co-op (ACPAV). Most appealing is Tana's *Caffè Italia* (1985), a history of Montreal's Italian community told through docudrama pieces (with Pierre Curzi in multiple roles) and rare archival footage.

The grasp of *genius loci*, the sense of occasion, the celebration of identity are the most clearly distinguishing marks of the French-language documentary tradition. When tied into a poetic sense of discovery and transformation, it links up with powerful trends within the French-language fictional film tradition too.

4

FICTIONAL FILMS IN FRENCH SINCE 1939

FROM FRANCE FILM TO RADIO-CANADA:
THE FIRST QUEBEC FILM INDUSTRY

A French-language film industry in Quebec needed good distribution, the removal of institutional barriers, and a pool of production talent. Cinema would be fifty years old before these conditions were met.

In the period of silent films translated versions were easy to provide: intertitles often appeared in both French and English consecutively during the same projection. But talkies changed that. Those, like Lionel Groulx, who worried about the moral climate fostered by the dominance of American films in Quebec could now extend their concern to the survival of the French language itself. During the thirties many local efforts were made to bring films from France to Quebec audiences. Beginning in 1932, the foremost among them was France Film, which assumed the patriotic mission of promoting and preserving the finest illustrations of French language film, and soon built a virtual monopoly of French-language distribution backed up by a network of theatres. It even claimed a part in the French production of *Maria Chapdelaine* (J. Duvivier, 1934), shot partly on location around Lac St-Jean and falsely touted as the first French-Canadian talking picture.

The Catholic Church and other conservative forces fought against film, which they identified with Hollywood, Mammon, and English domination. When 78 children perished in the 1927 fire at Montreal's Laurier Palace cinema, the ensuing outcry helped intensify film censorship and led to a ban on filmgoing for minors. But in the 1936 papal encyclical *Vigilanti Cura* the Church of Rome showed an openness to film that changed attitudes in Quebec. Resistance began to soften and by the 1940s the Church itself became a force in Quebec feature production.

The third requirement, a pool of suitable talent, came with the spread of French-language radio throughout Quebec in the 1930s and the consolidation in 1936 of national radio in Canada through the CBC. From 1931 Quebec radio stations began broadcasting plays, series, and serials in French, often emphasizing French-Canadian themes and settings. Many writers—Robert Choquette, Henry Deyglun, Claude-Henri Grignon, Gratien Gélinas and Jean Desprez—and performers initiated or consolidated careers in this medium. When the film industry began, the expertise was there: writers for the intimate dialogues suitable to the studio, players accustomed to the voice styles appropriate for microphones, and musicians who could provide incidental music for drama.

The Church moved first with a film promoting missionary recruitment. Jean-Marie Poitevin's *A la croisée des chemins* (1943) combined his religious morality play with documentary footage from his missionary years in China. **Paul Guèvremont**, a radio director at CKAC, was brought in to direct and star as the young man who receives the call and heeds it, abandoning the prospects of a successful career and marriage. The 16 mm. film circulated throughout the province's *collèges classiques*, convents, parish halls, and ciné-clubs.

From 1944 to 1953 fifteen original French features and four English films were produced in Quebec. Two companies—Renaissance and Québec Productions—built studios in the Montreal area and most of the films were produced by them or at their studios. Few are remembered outside Quebec, although some still appear on late-night French-language TV. They have encountered a recent spate of critical interest—mainly from cultural and social historians of popular culture. Of the four from Renaissance Films (and its successors), the first—*Le père Chopin* (Fédor Ozep, 1944)—is the best example. Two brothers from France, Paul and Pierre Dupont, have settled in Quebec. Paul is a church organist and music teacher (the film's title is his nickname) and lives with a family of five in a small village; bachelor Pierre is a businessman in the city. Anxious to renew ties with the family, Pierre brings them all to town, and the family soon begins to disintegrate.

Pierre undergoes a redemptive change of heart and the family is reunited at a concert conducted by Paul.

The seven films from Québec Productions are best remembered for a trio of films directed by Loïc Le Gouriadec (1888–1974), under his stage name **Paul Gury**. *Un homme et son péché* (1948), *Séraphin* (1949), and *Le curé de village* (1949) are three rural dramas adapted from radio serials of the thirties. *Un homme et son péché* (and its sequel *Séraphin*) drew on the 1933 novel by Claude-Henri Grignon that inspired the epic serial of the same name (1939–1962). *Le curé de village* drew on Robert Choquette's 1936 radio-play—also serialized in the thirties and revived on the release of the film for another series until 1955. More stylish than the other Quebec films, they contain many of the icons and recurrent themes of the era: rural folk under attack from a sinister stranger or an acquisitive antagonist—especially Grignon's legendary miser Séraphin; a heroine isolated from or bereft of family; conflict between the letter of the law and the sense of community; and above all, the benign wisdom of the village priest, everyone's mediator and father confessor. But the old values are occasionally undermined: Choquette's priest gives money and references to a youth leaving for the city; Séraphin gets his deserts when the villagers resort to the miser's own tricks and values.

Among the independent productions two stand out. *La petite Aurore l'enfant martyre* (**Jean-Yves Bigras**, 1951) was the last manifestation of an astonishing three-decade obsession. The prolonged child-abuse case ending with the murder of eleven-year-old Aurore by her stepmother occasioned a celebrated Quebec trial in 1920; from the trial a melodrama was developed and performed by an itinerant theatrical troupe. The play, unpublished until 1982, became the most prodigious success of Quebec's popular theatre. It was performed more than 5,000 times over thirty years. In 1951 Emile Asselin wrote a novel that grew into the script of the equally popular film. As a portrayal of traditional rural values the film is not typical fare, with its home-grown monster and a seemingly powerless country priest; it has more in common with fairytales of wicked stepmothers. Writer Jacques Ferron saw in it an allegory of Quebec herself: the mother-earth, now become stepmother to her orphaned, exiled children. The orphan 'exiled in his own land' would return for Ferron in Gratien Gélinas' Tit-Coq.

Gratien Gélinas had not only made his name as an actor on stage and radio—in the serial version of *Le curé de village*, for example—but he had been developing his own music-hall character, Fridolin, blending humour and pathos in a French-Canadian Chaplin. From 1938 to 1946, Gélinas annually staged *Fridolinons*, a revue based on this role, and in 1942 three of its sketches were filmed on stage and eventually combined to make the feature-length *Fridolin* (1944). In 1948 Gélinas transformed Fridolin—now illegitimate, orphaned and conscripted—into his most memorable creation. Within five years it too had become a film—*Tit-Coq* (Delacroix & Gélinas, 1953)—with Gélinas playing the role he had created on stage. Obsessed by his own bastardy and isolation, Tit-Coq is offered the promise of love and family with Marie-Ange before the army whisks him off to the European war—which separates him from her forever. Gélinas's popularization of the little man, presented in the street vernacular of Montreal, may have closed one period of Quebec film-making, but it clearly anticipated a new one that featured Michel Tremblay and a plethora of orphaned exiles with the gift of the gab.

When television came along and swallowed up the talents spawned by the first Quebec film industry, the two major production companies had died; both *Aurore* and *Tit-Coq* were produced by companies of convenience. The imported directors left; Paul Gury went to radio and Bigras to television. Of the writers, Grignon extended his radio and film successes with the hugely popular TV serial *Les belles histoire du pays d'en haut* (1956–73) and Choquette followed suit. But if television killed the first feature-film generation, it breathed life into the second.

QUEBEC'S NEW WAVE & FOUR *AUTEURS*

Despite a number of early short dramas in French—including Palardy's *L'homme aux oiseaux* (1952) from Roger Lemelin's light-hearted script of life in Quebec City's lower town—it was some years after the coming of television that the first series of full-length dramas was launched with the 26-part 'Panoramique' (1957–59). Grouped into six mini-series, the plots were set in critical moments of Quebec's recent social history. Three dealt with rural themes: the agricultural settlement of Abitibi in the Depression (*Les Brûlés*, Devlin, 1957–9), postwar rural life (*Le maître du Pérou*, F. Dansereau, 1958), and the experience of a mining inspector who quits his job to go 'wildcat' prospecting in the north (*Pays neuf*, F. Dansereau, 1958). The other three had urban settings: the wartime conscription crisis in a working-class Montreal family (*Il était une guerre*, Portugais, 1958), the growth of trade-union militancy in a strike during the 1940s (*Les 90 jours*, Louis Portugais, 1958–9), and the exploitation of office-workers (*Les mains nettes*, Jutra, 1958). But although the recent (urban) past was now furnishing dramatic material, the 'Panoramique' series, designed for episodic viewing on TV and only later trimmed into compact 16-mm. versions, was a transitional stage. The breakthrough to theatrical features came quite unofficially.

The new documentarists of the NFB's French-language units were gaining recognition on the festival circuits, and strong support from two new Quebec film journals: the Catholic *Séquences*, and the independent *Objectif*. Designed for the ciné-club public, these journals adopted the auteurist emphasis of their French contemporaries, publishing interviews with directors and thematic studies on local and international cinema. Because a director's films could be viewed as a coherent body of work, makers of short documentaries lionized by such critics could envisage feature films based on that reputation. Indeed the Quebec critics, emulating their counterparts in France, soon began making films too.

From 1963 to 1965, Claude Jutra, Gilles Groulx, Gilles Carle, and Jean-Pierre Lefebvre made their first theatrical features. These four became the core of the New Wave *auteurs* and their work showed both a personal vision and a profound commitment to the new Quebec. The films were black and white low-budget productions in the $30,000 to $65,000 range—two grew clandestinely from shorter NFB documentary projects and two were made privately—and amassed Festival awards in grand style. The directors all won Grand Prix awards at the Montreal Festival from 1963 to 1966, although it was Lefebvre's third feature that won (*Il ne faut pas mourir pour ça*)—his first having won at Pesaro after a refusal at Montreal. Jutra's *A tout prendre* (1963) was the landmark film. It brought together a direct style (synchronous sound, hand-held camera, available lighting, improvised dialogues), a personal voice (autobiographical material, confessional voice-over, fantasy-sequences), independent production (borrowed

equipment, volunteer crew, and personal financing) and an intellec-
tualism that was poles apart from the popular culture and the commercial
cinema of the day. The central character, Jutra himself, relived the
rise and fall of a love affair with the Haitian Johanne Harelle, also
played by herself. Easily the most intimate, self-indulgent film made
by the Quebec auteurs, it now has a darker irony because the final
shot of Jutra walking off the end of a pier into the St Lawrence River
prefigured his eventual death in 1987. Groulx's *Le chat dans le sac*
(1964) began as a short on the Québécois response to winter, but
secretly grew into a study of Claude (Godbout), the Quebec intellectual
in transition who gradually drifts away from an attachment to Barbara
(Ulrich), his Jewish anglophone girlfriend whose budding theatrical
career absorbs her more than Claude's problems of social and cultural
identity. Called 'the image of our most recent awakenings', Groulx's
film drew inspiration from Godard's *Vivre sa vie* (1962). Its discon-
tinuous editing style and refusal to allow the conventions of drama to
deflect attention from the spoken word demanded reflection and
interpretation from the audience.

A short on snow clearance grew into Carle's *La vie heureuse de
Léopold Z* (1965), a series of sketches from the Christmas eve of
Leopold Z. Tremblay (Guy L'Ecuyer), a snowplough operator in
Montreal. Overcoming one obstacle after another—a storm and calls
to work, the arrival of an out-of-town cousin to sing in a night-club,
the acquisition of a loan and the purchase of his wife's Christmas
fur coat, his son's choir-practice—he reaches the Basilica of Notre-
Dame just in time for midnight mass; family ritual survives extraneous
distractions and the demands of work. For *Le Révolutionnaire* (1965)
Lefebvre and his colleagues from the film journal *Objectif* went up to
a farmhouse and shot the film in a week. A sardonic fable of the mood
of half-cocked revolution that Lefebvre perceived in Quebec, it showed
a band of revolutionaries dashing off to the country for guerilla training, only to end up killing each other instead. The stylization, the
self-conscious musical three-part structure, the dislocation of tones
(burlesque, lyricism, and pathos are intertwined disconcertingly) and
the experimental effects (Pierre Hébert's images and word-balloons
scratched on the film) combined to produce a genuinely original
style.

Although schooled in documentary at the NFB (in Lefebvre's case, deeply influenced by it), the four combined an interest in poetry and the stage that complemented their dispassionate vision as observers and imbued it with a type of poetic realism associated with Jean Renoir and Marcel Carné. Their irony and irreverence, their profound respect for film culture and their loose plotting marked their affinities with the French New Wave of the early sixties. But in their hopes that artistic expression could provide a magical release from the fear and self-loathing of Quebec's 'dark ages', they are allied—some more closely than others—with Paul-Emile Borduas' surrealist *Refus Global* of 1948.

In the films of **Claude Jutra** the magical release and allegories of a new vision often come through tales of adolescence or emotional disturbance. The hybrid *WOW* (NFB, 1969) combined talks with nine teenagers on their views of modern life with short sequences illustrating their dreams. *Mon oncle Antoine* (NFB, 1971) grew from Clément Perron's script recalling his childhood in a Quebec mining town of the 1940s. Set at Christmas-time, it showed a young Benoît gradually losing his allusions about the adult world he had previously held in awe—a world represented mainly by his uncle Antoine, the town storekeeper and undertaker who is ultimately revealed as incompetent, a drunk, and a cuckold. Benoît's rebellion begins with the snowball he hurls at the town boss who throws Christmas gifts from his sleigh on a progress through the main street.

In the Toronto period of Jutra's career, when he made films for the CBC and directed two Beryl Fox productions, his interest in vulnerable inner worlds of marvels shifted to visions of mental disturbance with *Ada* (1977), the adaptation of a Margaret Gibson short story of life in a mental hospital, and *Dreamspeaker* (1977), about an emotionally-disturbed boy who escapes to live with an Indian shaman. The worlds of childhood and madness came together most powerfully in Jutra's last film *La dame en couleurs* / *Lady of Colours* (1985), a powerful, macabre portrayal of life in an asylum: a group of orphans, brought in to help the nuns, explore the secret labyrynthine passages under the building and, accompanied by an epileptic painter, create a world of forbidden games, rituals, and dreams.

Jutra has frequently returned to the ups and downs of the male-female couple, which critics have linked to his revelation of his homosexuality in *A tout prendre*. *Kamouraska* (1973), from Anne

Hébert's 1970 novel set in nineteenth-century Quebec, was a sumptuous period piece: Élisabeth d'Aulnières (Geneviève Bujold), at her second husband's deathbed, relives in a series of flashbacks a passionate past in which a stormy love affair led to the murder of her first husband, the brutish seigneur of Kamouraska. In *Pour le meilleur et pour le pire* (1975), Jutra and Monique Mercure played scenes from a middle-class marriage in Montreal. *By Design* (1980), set in the world of fashion design, was a gentle comedy about a lesbian couple's attempts to have a baby.

Jutra's films often show quirks of rhythm and structure that have perplexed some critics: the shift in *Mon oncle Antoine* from the light-hearted action around the uncle's store to a slower, graver, lyrical section in which Antoine's sleighride with his nephew to collect a child's body for burial serves as the passage to a new awareness for Benoît; the blatant dislocation of time-cycles in *Pour le meilleur et le pire*, in which twenty-four hours in the life of the couple coincide with a cycle of four seasons outside their house and sixteen years in the life of their daughter. In the same film Jutra also played with the alternation of monochrome and colour—and even included a song and dance sequence.

Jutra's death in 1987 came as a sad and premature end to an enigmatic director's career that was divided between a Quebec that blew hot and cold about his films and an English Canada that welcomed him and gave him work for half a decade. The Toronto interlude weakened the homogeneity of vision and style associated with an *auteur*'s work, but a thorough revaluation of his complete work could change that assessment. It will take time for Jutra's film work to receive appropriate weight in the historical record of Canadian film (the full three-hour version of *Kamouraska* only appeared in 1983 through Pay-TV), but there is no doubt that he has given us at least one of its masterpieces. In 1984 the organizers of the Toronto Festival of Festivals polled Canadian film scholars and critics for a 'Best Ten' list of Canadian films: *Mon oncle Antoine* topped the list.

Gilles Groulx's fictional film career since *Le chat dans le sac* has been even more sporadic than Jutra's. *Où êtes-vous donc?* (1968) began as a documentary on popular song in the new Quebec and over three years evolved into a story illustrating different directions popular music could take, represented by three Quebec singers: Georges

Dor (the poet using song to express the desire for a better world), Christian (opting for a pop-singer's career), and Mouffe (whose songs are used in commercials). From the distant, lonely reaches of the North Shore they gradually drift down to the modern city. The film uses a wide variety of formalizing devices, playing with colour and monochrome, inserting slogans and printed texts along with various manifestations of the sounds and music of our era in a dense collage. *Entre tu et vous* (1969) went further along the path followed by Godard in France, rejecting plot in favour of a series of symbolic demonstrations by Pierre Harel and Paule Baillargeon of contemporary life and its sources of alienation. Recently Groulx, after censorship troubles at the NFB and a serious accident, made *Au pays de Zom* (1982), whose denunciation of modern capitalist society took the form of a surrealist musical fantasy.

Gilles Carle's fictional features, privately produced since his first NFB escapade, have expanded from the satirical low-budget *Le viol d'une jeune fille douce* (1968) to the film-cum-TV spectaculars, *Les Plouffe* (1981) and *Maria Chapdelaine* (1983). Until his recent adaptations, the films often showed a protagonist, variously victimized or exploited in the city, who seeks authentic values, hidden truths, or redress beyond the city; a rude awakening or failure is the outcome, since the forces of exploitation dwell in the countryside too. In Carle's masterpiece, *La vraie nature de Bernadette* (1972), the 'saintly' heroine leaves her middle-class urban marriage and comforts in search of communal life, sexual liberation, and love of nature—only to find the farmers economically exploited, and herself sexually exploited by men and harrassed by religious fanatics who take her for a saint after an apparently miraculous cure. She finally joins the farmers' protest and chases away the pilgrims.

Carle's films are a display-case for the fantasies, formative myths, and political preoccupations of the artistic intelligentsia of his generation in Quebec. The heterogeneity of the work recalls the surrealists' refusal of fixed genres and their interlacing of laughter, fear, and desire in order to discomfit the bourgeois spectator seeking relaxation and certainty. Allegorical and rhetorical devices proliferate. Cycles of exploitation are bound into recurrent imagery, such as the wood and paper products in *La Mort d'un bûcheron*, or the small town brothel that serves as a microcosm of the world on the brink of World

War II in *Les corps célestes* (1973). There are also echoes of the music-hall, with its loose affiliation of comic sketches, spectacle, sentimental entertainment, and erotica; a travelling music-hall is actually the centre of action in *Fantastica* (1980). By blurring the distinction between spectacle and *film à thèse*, Carle has infuriated many critics. Can Carle's use of women as exemplars of contemporary forms of exploitation—Carole Laure as topless singer and nude model in *La Mort d'un bûcheron*, for instance—be separated from their appropriation as the titillating object of the prurient male gaze? The answer is that the distinction is neither made nor sought. Carle does not always acknowledge the appeal Carole Laure's body may have for part of his viewing public, but the context for its display lies in meanings that transcend prurience while retaining the erotic shiver.

If **Jean-Pierre Lefebvre**'s films are known in English-speaking circles, it is thanks to festival recognition and scholars like Peter Harcourt. But it has been a long time coming. The first to gain commercial release in English Canada, although a number were dubbed for TV, was his nineteenth feature, *Le jour S* (1983). Lefebvre has always believed that films made for a small Quebec audience should be budgeted accordingly. Mostly shot in 16 mm., more than half of them cost less than $100,000 and none reached a budget of $500,000. After five independent features, Lefebvre made two at the NFB (1967–68) and established a new directors' program. Finding the in-house atmosphere too claustrophobic there, he has since worked through his own company, Cinak.

Lefebvre felt that the Québécois 'must each feel poetically and politically responsible' for their collective fate. Art and politics would be aligned in the spirit of Breton's second surrealist manifesto and Borduas' *Refus global*. But Lefebvre's films do not offer unequivocal dreams of liberation or self-realization. More often they portray promising beginnings, false hopes, and momentary irruptions and epiphanies, along with self-destructive inertia and a sense of eternal return. Defying recognized critical categories, they present unsynthesized juxtapositions of clashing moods, styles, genres, and meanings.

Since *Le révolutionnaire* (1965), Lefebvre has made eighteen feature films. Peter Harcourt divided them into the 'esoteric' and the 'exoteric', and there is no doubt that some of them are far more accessible to a broad public than others—those with strong story-lines, such as *Le vieux pays où Rimbaud est mort* (1977), as opposed to those containing long, dense poetic reflections, such as *Ultimatum* (1973). In their *Dictionnaire du cinéma québécois*, Houle and Julien proposed another division: the intimist works, including conversation-pieces such as *Mon amie Pierrette* (NFB, 1967), in which the philosopher-artist Raoul Duguay (played by himself) cheekily disrupts a family's desultory weekend at the cottage, or *Les dernières fiançailles* (1973), a lyrical portrait of the last days in the life of an elderly rural couple; and the works of protest, such as *Jusqu'au coeur* (NFB, 1968), an allegory in which Robert Charlebois is being programmed for war, commercials, and conformity, or *Un succès commercial* (1969), in which Lefebvre lampoons the vogue for Quebec soft-core pornography at the time. Some of his films were more personal and dealt with his views about film-making: *Le gars des vues* (1976), which paid homage to amateur film-makers in a discussion piece about the nature of film, and *Au rythme de mon coeur* (1983), a film diary made while Lefebvre was travelling across Canada with a retrospective of his films and was faced with the sudden death of Marguerite Duparc, his wife and lifelong collaborator. But his films contain interludes and episodes of each of these approaches and Lefebvre has always claimed to be seeking a dialectical progression from film to film, making each a distinct work.

Lefebvre often reveals structure, breaking his films into clearly defined parts (usually three or four), giving chapter headings and distinct formal characteristics to each segment. Extremely long takes force us to experience time as the characters do. Formal and technical features often draw attention to themselves: the interplay of colour and monochrome, the studied co-ordination of colours, stylized camera movements. Such features as chapterization and *plans-séquences* have been traced to the influence of Jean-Luc Godard, but other critics found their antecedents in the little-known *Les Désœuvrés* (1959), **René Bail**'s independently-made direct-style account of a group of bored adolescents and their escapade with a 'borrowed' truck. Many Quebec critics, including Lefebvre, placed this film in the pantheon of essential Quebec cinema. Lefebvre has said that his films take on the shape proper to their subject-matter, and his Romantic desire to embody and correlate—to fuse the forms of telling with the forms of the told—extends to the scripts, which abound with clues linking the specific to the general and binding portraits of individuals and couples to Lefebvre's vision of Quebec, and to a broader vision of the contemporary human condition.

Lefebvre's as yet unfinished trilogy may be his master work. *Il ne faut pas mourir pour ça* (NFB, 1967) introduces us to Abel (Marcel Sabourin), a genial eccentric who keeps books in the refrigerator, his thoughts on a chalkboard, and model planes in bird-cages. His life seems to unfold according to some distant fate—a chance call in a pay-phone, with an unknown girl bemoaning her fate, oddly prefigures Abel's own day, as his mother dies and a former girl-friend leaves for Paris to be married. *Le vieux pays où Rimbaud est mort* (1977) sees Abel visiting France and discovering that what he had learnt about the old country no longer holds true. He meets Jeanne, a garment-worker whom he accompanies to the northern industrial town of Charleville (Rimbaud's birthplace) for her mother's funeral, and Anne, a professional woman he joins in Marseille (Rimbaud's deathplace) for a short affair during a crisis in her marriage. The third film is tentatively titled *La mort du père Prodigue*. These films hold the essence of Lefebvre's off-key blend of poetry, reflection, and revelation that has long been known to his admirers.

OTHER GRADUATES FROM THE GOLDEN AGE OF QUEBEC DOCUMENTARY

Many cinéastes who made their name with NFB documentaries, whether direct style or not, joined the wave of sixties features. The thematic and stylistic characteristics of their earlier work carried over into their fictional films.

Raymond Garceau, the major NFB social documentarist of Quebec's rural life and history, dwelt on the impact of rural change in three NFB fictional features: *Le grand Rock* (1967), *Vive la France* (1970), and *Et du fils* (1971). *Le grand Rock*, a Québécois Western, traced a young trapper's gradual corruption by urban life, the cash nexus, and the consumer society—typified by his ill-fated marriage to an acquisitive cashier and his drift into crime and violence. In a Quebec excited by reform and modernization, many people were not ready for Garceau's regrets. His features were poorly received and Garceau returned to documentary.

Clément Perron, who showed the frustrations of small town life in documentary and in his script for *Mon oncle Antoine*, portrayed small towns in the Beauce for his own NFB fictional features: *Taureau* (1973), which dwelt on the bigoted reaction of the townsfolk to an affair between the amicable, retarded protagonist of the title (André Melançon) and the local schoolmistress; and *Partis pour la gloire* (1975), which depicted local attitudes to the tracking down of conscientious objectors by the Military Police during the 1942 conscription crisis. In each film, individual acts of revolt against a distant establishment with remote objectives occur within a repressive, closed society. Earlier, Perron had co-directed *C'est pas la faute à J. C.* (NFB, 1967) with cameraman **Georges Dufaux**, a light comedy in the spirit of the documentary *Québec-USA* , about a guided tour of the province with three Americans.

Cinematographers and sound technicians, whose alert eyes and ears had contributed so much to the sensibility of the *cinéma direct* approach, extended this interest into their fictional films. **Michel Brault**'s *Entre la mer et l'eau douce* (1967) was later compared to Don Shebib's *Goin' Down the Road* (1970) for its semi-documentary portrayal of a young man migrating to the city. But he made it with Pierre Patry's Co-opératio, who wanted it shot in the commercial 35-mm. gauge. The heavier equipment compromised Brault's observational style, although not in all scenes. Brault had to wait for his second feature project, *Les ordres* (1974), to attempt a synthesis of fiction and the direct style. Based on the recorded experiences of some fifty Quebec detainees in the 1970 October Crisis, the script follows five disparate characters who are bundled off to prison at dawn without knowing the reason or their ultimate fate—one even undergoes a simulated execution. From *cinéma direct* Brault used a highly mobile camera, available light in enclosed settings, synchronous sound, compilational editing, and so on. But he also drew attention to the conventions of drama. The actors introduce themselves and their characters on camera and can be heard later in voice-over commentary. Brault contrasted a chilling desaturated colour for the prison sequences with black and white for the rest. The film did well in Canada and beyond (four **CFA**s; Best Director's Prize at Cannes), but in Quebec some felt that Brault's humanist denunciation of an impersonal system played down the political struggle and deflected attention from more radical criticism.

Recent social history also furnished material for **Jean-Claude Labrecque**'s *Les Smattes* (1972), which shows the two Pilon brothers (Donald and Daniel) on the run through the bush against a background of the Quebec government's resettlement of depressed villages in the Gaspé peninsula. Labrecque's unfinished trilogy—*Les vautours* (1975) and *Les années de rêve* (1984) to date—traces the life of Louis Pelletier (Gilbert Sicotte) from the declining years of the Duplessis era, in which his own emancipation from the grip of his family coincides with Quebec's release from Duplessis, to the 1970 crisis (by the end of the second film) and political activism, which draws Louis into family tragedy and the traumatic October round-up. Labrecque also made *L'affaire Coffin* (1979), a docudrama on Wilbert Coffin, the anglophone prospector from Gaspé who was accused, condemned, and executed for the murder of three American hunters in 1953. Cameraman **Thomas Vamos** made two films centred on reporters, in a sense dramatizing the documentarist himself. In *L'exil* (NFB, 1971) a reporter under pressure for his outspoken investigating takes his girlfriend and a camper into 'exile' in the Laurentian northwoods, only to stumble on evidence of a secret military take-over. In *La fleur aux dents* (NFB, 1975) a radio host obsessively collects memorabilia and sound material about the 'Quiet Revolution' while his wife and daughter start changing their lives for reasons he does not understand.

Fernand Dansereau's *Le Festin des morts* / *Mission of Fear* (1964), the NFB's first 'official' feature film, and soundman **Marcel Carrière's** *St-Denis dans le temps* (NFB, 1969) may be compared as historical reconstitutions. Dansereau's drama of life among missionaries in seventeenth century Huronia derived its script from the Jesuit *Relations* and was shot in a specially built replica of a Huron Indian village. Made in a brooding Bergmanesque style, the film dramatized the clash of two cultures and the inner doubts of a young priest on his first mission. Despite two **CFA**s—including Best Feature—the film was excoriated by critics like *Objectif*'s Jean-Pierre Lefebvre for over-direction, theatrical acting, and historical stereotyping. In *St-Denis dans le temps*, the anniversary of the Patriotes' 1837 victory over British forces at Saint-Denis leads to the intercutting of scenes from that rebellion with scenes of unrest in 1960s Quebec, while the revolutionary Marie-Claire engages in debate with the pragmatic Gilles. The living documentary style of the historic scenes is closer to that of the British *Culloden* (Watkins, 1964) than to Dansereau's. Both Dansereau and Carrière have changed direction in later features. In *O.K. Laliberté* (NFB, 1973) and *Ti-Mine, Bernie pis la gang* (NFB, 1976) Carrière combined the documentarist's attention to detail with a spontaneous acting style in two light comedies about working-class characters. Dansereau's growing interest in film for social projects lay behind two films: in *Tout l'temps, tout l'temps, tout l'temps* (Dansereau, NFB, 1969) the film-makers developed the script, shot the film, and edited it all in co-operation with a Montreal working-class cast, who played out a psycho-drama of a dispersed city family's reunion in their old country home; and in *Thetford au milieu de notre vie* (1978), with **Iolande Rossignol**, two years' collaboration with workers' families in Thetford Mines was worked into a professionally acted drama about the oppressive weight of the mine on a family's life as the mother suffers the frustrations of trying to re-enter the labour force.

After the short feature *La neige a fondu sur le Manicouagan* (NFB, 1965), showing a crisis in the marriage of a dam-worker in a northern hydro project, **Arthur Lamothe** made his first full-length drama at Co-opératio: *Poussière sur la ville* (1965), a gloomy adaptation of André Langevin's gloomy novel. After the lengthy series on native peoples (see Chapter 3), Lamothe returned to drama with *Equinoxe* (1986), a story of an old man's return with his granddaughter to the St Lawrence island where, in his youth, he had been betrayed into prison and exile.

Jacques Godbout's earlier work often combined an interest in popular culture and self-referentiality. After *YUL 871* (NFB, 1966), an unsuccessful France-Canada co-production, he made the transitional *Kid Sentiment* (NFB, 1968), working with a group of Outremont adolescents to improvise a loosely structured story; the middle third was a discussion with the participants about the film. His *Ixe-13* (NFB, 1971) self-consciously used musical-comedy conventions to pay homage to the pop-culture of post-war French Canada in a story about the spy from Pierre Saurel's weekly serial of the forties. With *La gammick* (NFB, 1974) Godbout transformed another genre, the crime thriller, into a critical study of contemporary Quebec society.

THE POPULAR ENTERTAINERS

Co-opératio, founded in 1963 by Roger Blais, Pierre Patry and Jean-Claude Lord, produced seven features in five years, including the first by Lamothe and Brault and three by **Pierre Patry**—best represented by *Trouble-Fête* (1964), the tale of a Quebec rebel without a cause. The most prolific fictional feature director to come from the group is Lord, whose films—box-office potboilers, international co-productions, and television—have cannily followed the trends of government programs in support of Canadian feature film production.

After adapting Claude Jasmin's *Délivrez-nous du mal* (1965) for Co-opératio, **Jean-Claude Lord** entered the commercial private sector, chiefly with producers Pierre David and Claude Héroux. With the early films such as *Les Colombes* (1970) that he wrote, directed, and edited himself, critics greeted him as a new *auteur*, but he has evolved into a Hollywood- style professional with films that exploit contemporary issues more for dramatic potential than as a basis for reflection. The successful *Bingo* (1974) concentrated on political terrorism and the state's oppressive reponse, to suggest that violent protest plays into the hands of the extreme right; *Parlez-nous d'amour* (1976) denounced the shallow and corrupt world of TV show business; *Panique* (1977) fed our worst fears of industrial pollution. Lord has since made genre films with big budgets, an English-language cast, and an eye to the international market: a psychopathic killer-thriller (*Visiting Hours* ,1981); a romantic comedy with high production values (*Cover Girls*, 1982); a mad scientist suspense thriller (*The Vindicator*, 1984); and a family adventure (*Toby McTeague*, 1985). Recently he directed *Lance et compte / He Shoots He Scores* (1986), the CBC TV serial about a young ice-hockey professional. Lord's films are glossily photographed, recently by René Verzier; the action and the editing are brisk; the music is dramatic and intrusive.

In Quebec from 1968 to 1974 a dozen or so films were made to take advantage of less stringent censorship of sex. Known as 'films de fesses' in French and 'maple-syrup porno' in *Variety*, they were promoted not in the name of sexual liberation but as a way of localizing images of sexuality—what Denis Héroux called undressing 'la petite Québécoise'. They were also to provide a commercial base for the Quebec film industry, much as Roger Vadim and Brigitte Bardot had done for the French New Wave with *Et Dieu créa la femme* in 1956. The chief exponents of the trend were **Denis Héroux** and **Claude Fournier**. Their films follow two patterns: the earnest drama of sexual escapade and return, exemplified by Denis Héroux's *Valérie* (1968), in which a convent-girl breaks out on a biker's pillion, joins a hippie commune, becomes a topless dancer, and works the streets before falling for a sensitive widower and son who provide a ready-made family and a safe return to conventionality; or the bawdy romp of Claude Fournier's *Deux femmes en or* (1970), which tells the story of two bored suburban housewives who decide to amuse themselves by the systematic seduction of house-callers. Fournier's films mix popular actors and musicians, scabrous humour, and titillating sex to secure the commercial success that Lefebvre decried in his *Un succès commercial*. Like sitcoms, they have an episodic, formulaic construction and conclude with the triumph of the central characters. Over the years Héroux and Fournier have tapped popular trends with films featuring pop-singers and teenage idols as well as slapstick comedy. Each tried, disastrously, to break out of the mould with a historical epic—*Quelques arpents de neige* (Héroux, 1972), set in the 1837 Rebellion in Lower Canada, and *Alien Thunder* (Fournier, 1973), starring Donald Sutherland, about the 1897 incident at Duck Lake, Saskatchewan that pitted an Indian fugitive against the Northwest Mounted Police.

Some critics have been perplexed by the two Fourniers—the sensitive documentarist of the NFB and New York's *cinéma-vérité* group of Drew Associates, and the maker of exploitation flicks—but Fournier always had mass audience tastes in mind, whether introducing the NFB intellectuals to pro wrestling (*La Lutte*, 1961), bringing two popular comediennes like Denise Filiatrault and Dominique Michel together in a sex-comedy (*Je suis loin de toi, mignonne* 1976), or casting a well-known hard-core pornography actor as the puritanical new head of a police vice-squad (*Les Chiens chauds / Cops and Other Lovers*, 1979). It then came as a shock when Fournier began work with Gabrielle Roy's blessing on the adaptation of her 1945 novel *Bonheur d'occasion* (1982). As a super-production, it had theatrical and television versions—the latter a longer mini-series—and was shot bilingually with the same performers in English and French. Reviews were divided. The adaptation was praised by those who saw the interaction of the characters and the story of Florentine's search for security and love in wartime Montreal as the essential elements of the novel; the acting drew applause and Marilyn Lightstone, as the long-suffering mother, won an award at Moscow. But the film dismayed those who thought it trivialized the strong social criticism embedded in the novel by producing a glossy soap-opera that simplified characters and presented psychological conflicts melodramatically.

FROM OCTOBER CRISIS TO REFERENDUM: THE SEVENTIES

Many film-makers who began making fictional features in the seventies had not served an apprenticeship in NFB documentary or the *cinéma direct*. They were not graduates of the Quiet Revolution, and their early works did not burst with revolutionary enthusiasm. Their sense of the new Quebec and its independence movement was tempered by the trauma of the 1970 crisis and their films tended to dwell on the nature of domination and fear. Youth was not seen as a metaphor for a promising new future; attention shifted to marginal characters, the chronically unemployed, underground artists, petty criminals, vagrants, and drop-outs. The past was treated nostalgically or seen as a parade of disastrous models fated to recur through ignorance. Literary sources, often shunned in the heyday of *cinéma direct*, were exploited through adaptations of novels; new links were forged between film and theatre. Formal experimentation and the surreal cultivation of dream and fantasy continued, but with more sinister and pessimistic overtones than before.

Two film-makers who show many of these characteristics are **Denys Arcand** and **Jacques Leduc**. Although they *had* served an apprenticeship in documentary, it was not in the Griersonian or *direct* styles of the previous generations. Their documentariess were more like film-essays—tougher, more analytical, more accusatory, swaying from cynicism to pessimism—as in Arcand's features *Québec: Duplessis et après* (1972) and *Le confort et l'indifférence* (1981), where he blends contemporary news footage with historic re-enactments to show how the lessons of history have been forgotten, or in Leduc's *On est loin du soleil* (NFB, 1970). In the latter film the various elements of Brother André's life are re-cast as a series of stark portraits of the members of a Rosemont family—going about their everyday life, embodying the beatified Brother's spirit of resignation, self-sacrifice, and acceptance that conditioned the inertia of the masses in Quebec. Using extremely long takes (*plans-séquences*) and sparse plots reminiscent of Lefebvre's more personal style, Arcand and Leduc deconstructed traditional narratives and genres and presented a pessimistic, ironic view of society. By rooting the action in duration as experienced by the characters, they avoided the condensation of time typical of drama. By dismantling dramatic forms, Arcand focuses attention on questions of social and public morality: the corrosive effects of acquisitiveness in a consumer society in the gangster-film *La maudite galette* (1972); political corruption in *Réjeanne Padovani* (1973); company town alienation and political censorship in *Gina* (1974). Arcand's triumph is *Le déclin de l'empire américain* (1985). Ostensibly a series of witty conversations about sex among a group of Montreal academics going off to a lakeside cottage, it also dwells on history and models of historical explanation, evincing a collapse of faith in grand theory—a theme explored in his film-essays. After *On est loin du soleil*, Leduc made a moving demystification of everyday conjugal love, *Tendresse ordinaire* (NFB, 1973); the scenes of a woman passing time at home by the St Lawrence are intercut with shots of her husband on the long journey back from work in the north and flashbacks of times spent together. Following his hypnotic, minimalist series 'Chronique de la vie quotidienne' (NFB, 1977–78), shot in a similar style, Leduc's *Le dernier glacier* (NFB, 1984) shows the shutdown of the northern town of Schefferville, interlaced with scenes in the life of a family broken by the experience.

Compared with Arcand and Leduc, Jean Beaudin and Francis Mankiewicz have directed more accessible, traditional dramas. **Jean Beaudin**'s films have evolved from period-pieces stunningly photographed (by Pierre Mignot): *J.A. Martin photographe* (NFB, 1976), which followed the summer round of a turn-of-the-century travelling photographer; and *Cordélia* (NFB/Radio-Canada, 1979), which adapted Pauline Cadieux's account in *La lampe dans la fenêtre* of the 1897 trial and hanging of Cordélia Viau for her husband's murder. In both films Beaudin adopted a cellular structure of 'memory units' separated by fades to black, discreet camerawork, and underplayed acting that relied on glances and facial expression. Beaudin then

turned to literary adaptations with disturbingly sinister undertones—
Mario (1983) from Claude Jasmin's *La Sablière*; and *Le Matou* (1984)
from Yves Beauchemin's novel. Each featured a marginal child (one
an autistic boy, the other a street brat) in the title role and set their
parallel fantasy-world on a course towards self-destruction. Both the
marvellous and the fantastic abound: the children's Moorish fort built
of *objets trouvés* on the Magdalen Islands in *Mario*; the Mephistophe-
lian Ratablavatsky and his sidekick Len Slipskin, who get their
comeuppance from the young couple of restaurateurs in *Le Matou*.
Children also play an important role in **Francis Mankiewicz**'s films.
In *Le temps d'une chasse* (NFB, 1972), a low-key story about the
ritual of a weekend shooting trip, the boy observes the gradual strip-
ping away of the mythic, liberating qualities of the hunt and watches
the men drift by stages into degradation and catastrophe. After the
theatrical *Une amie d'enfance* (1977), Mankiewicz directed two films
from scripts by Réjean Ducharme: *Les bons débarras* (1980) and *Les
beaux souvenirs* (NFB, 1981). Each shows a young female protagonist
scheming to break the ties between her remaining parent and potential
competitors for love and affection. In *Les bons débarras*—the more
successful of the two (it received a shower of **CFA**s including Best
Picture)—the thirteen-year-old Manon's object of jealous affection is
her mother, who lives in cottage country with an older retarded son
and a policeman-boyfriend and sells firewood to the well-to-do. It is a
world upside-down: the adults play like children, the child talks and
behaves like an adult; the policeman is afraid of dogs. Well-acted and
sensitively photographed (by Michel Brault), Mankiewicz' best films
join Beaudin's as works in the Jutra tradition.

Jean-Pierre Lefebvre's 'First Works' program (1969–70) at the
NFB gave young directors a chance to work with professional crews.
These works sometimes show Lefebvre's influence, and were destined
more for art-houses than for a mass audience. **Fernand Bélanger**'s
short *Ti-Cœur* (1970) and his feature *Ty-Peupe* (1971) are interesting
relics of the sixties counter-culture; some of the same preoccupations
returned in *L'Émotion dissonante* (NFB, 1984), a sympathetic picture of the marijuana culture that mixed staged and documentary
sequences, and *Passiflora* (NFB, 1986), an anarchic compilation film
made with Dagmar Gueissaz-Teufel, about the simultaneous Montreal visits by Pope John Paul II and Michael Jackson. Following his

Jean-François Xavier de . . . (NFB, 1969), **Michel Audy** subsequently made *Corps et Ames* (1972) for Lefebvre's Cinak and *La Maison qui empêche de voir la ville* (1974) independently. Obscure and symbolic portrayals of bisexual triangles, they were all flops, although at least one gay critic has recently acclaimed them as landmarks in the development of gay film. **André Théberge**, a critic from *Objectif*, made *Question de vie* (1970), a portrait of a woman gradually succumbing to mental breakdown under the pressures of everyday routine, factory drudgery, and family collapse. He dealt more successfully with a similar theme in *La dernière neige* (1973), an adaptation of Jacques Ferron's mini-story 'Retour à Val d'Or' for the NFB series 'Toulmonde parle français'. **Jean Chabot**'s *Mon enfance à Montréal* (NFB, 1970), a study of the difficulties of a young working-class family adapting to a new life in the big city, is portrayed oneirically through the eyes of their young child. Chabot's attempted deconstruction of the police-thriller, *Une nuit en Amérique* (1974), failed both with the critics and at the box-office. Since then he has worked at the OFQ and the NFB where he eventually made *La fiction nucléaire* (1978), mixing genres and modes to denounce nuclear energy and northern energy development.

L'Association Co-opérative de Productions Audio-Visuelles (ACPAV), founded in 1971, also encouraged new works by young directors. It began with the first feature drama by a woman outside the NFB. **Mireille Dansereau**'s *La vie rêvée* (1972) showed two young women, who work for a film company, pursuing their fantasies of a perfect man until the discovery of their hero's real self frees them of this obsession. Dansereau encountered difficulties with ACPAV's male executive who wanted her film to articulate the feminist challenge analytically and politically and opposed what she called her 'intuitive, very emotional and personal approach'. The film mixed sequences of early memories, fantasies, advertising, and dreams to show that women's desire is constituted by images that are socially constructed. After working in Poirier's 'En tant que femmes' project on features anthologizing alternative attitudes to love, marriage, and family, Dansereau made *L'arrache-coeur* (1979), the portrait of a woman writer (Louise Marleau) caught in a web of conflicting loyalties to parents, husband, and young son. Here family influences and ties conflict with the woman's sense of her own identity; she needs to be freed from the overpowering influence of her mother. Dansereau's films show that her interest is in women's mental universe, not their material status. Also making a start with ACPAV was **Brigitte Sauriol**. Her films often deal with relationships in which women feel a trust has been betrayed. The short *Le loup blanc* (1973) portrays a woman's revenge when her boy-friend retreats to a shack in the Laurentian backwoods. Sauriol's first feature, *L'absence* (1975), shows the difficulties of a 30-year-old photographer Louise (Frédérique Collin) when her father returns after fifteen years away on a social mission with the native peoples, a desertion she cannot forgive even though her father is dying. *Rien qu'un jeu* (Ciné-groupe, 1983) is a story of father-daughter incest.

Also from ACPAV is **Jean-Guy Noël**'s black comedy *Tu brûles . . . tu brûles* (1973). A riposte to Garceau's *Le Grand Rock*, this was Noël's tribute to the post-sixties' drop-out generation. Guy L'Ecuyer plays the mayor and fire-chief of a little village in the Laurentians. His son Gabriel, also a fireman, has dropped out and lives in a mountain shack. When fire threatens the village community, a sequence of intercessors (sister, father, parish priest) climb the mountain seeking Gabriel's help but find him inflexible. The village burns down, his father dies, and Gabriel finally decides the way to freedom lies in Montreal. *Ti-cul Tougas* (1976) presents another dream of escape as two young musicians abscond to the Magdalen Islands with a government grant that belongs to a brass band touring the Maritimes. There they dream of California, and eventually begin their journey with a Country Music concert in New England. *Contrecœur* (1980), made for Pierre Lamy, again shows a small group opting for life on the road in the face of the complexities of small-town existence and family life; the town is ironically named Contrecœur ('reluctance').

André Forcier has been compared to René Bail, Jean Vigo, Milos Foreman, and Réjean Ducharme. After a poorly-received first independent feature, *Le retour de l'Immaculée Conception* (1971), Forcier made his reputation with *Bar salon* (1973), a series of slices of life in a seedy bar going out of business that conveys an atmosphere reminiscent of Czech films of the sixties. *L'eau chaude, l'eau frette* (ACPAV, 1976) shows 24 hours in a Montreal rooming-house, including a party that brings together a thoroughly eccentric group of marginals. *Au clair de la lune* (1982) follows the albino trickster Frank and the arthritic ex-bowling champion Bert into the back streets of Montreal's inner city while a mysterious campaign of tire-slashing takes place around the green Chevrolet where they sleep.

Since Gratien Gélinas' films, the stage and the cinema have come together more often for television than for the theatre screen. In the seventies **André Brassard**'s *Il était une fois dans l'est* (1973) brought together many of the familiar scenes and social outcasts of Michel Tremblay's plays: the working-class housewives and waitresses of Montreal's East End alongside the gays, lesbians, and transvestites of the bars on 'the Main' (Montreal's rue Saint-Laurent). In *Le soleil se lève en retard* (1976) Brassard and Tremblay tell the simple story of two sisters: one gradually moves into marriage as the other's marriage is cruelly brought to an end.

Pascal Gélinas made *Montréal Blues* (1972) with the experimental troupe Le Grand Cirque Ordinaire, which he had known and worked with for some years. The script, written co-operatively and developed on video, told of a series of romantic attachments between the members of a touring stage show and the people who work in an organic food restaurant that gave its name to the film. **Paule Baillargeon**, an actress from the same acting troupe, made a short—*Anastasie Oh! ma chérie* (1977), about a woman forced into rehabilitation after retreating into solitude from her family—before making the experimental *La cuisine rouge* (with Frédérique Collin, 1980), using techniques and actors from Le Grand Cirque Ordinaire. The filmscript, also developed from improvisational workshops on video, showed a wedding reception in a cheap restaurant-bar that goes awry when the women there refuse to undertake their traditional tasks and the men respond with immobility and confusion. Baillargeon's films are typified by theatrical mise-en-scène, minimalist representation, stylized acting, and long takes, features they share with the films of Lefebvre and with neo-Brechtian theatre, but that here are made to serve a radical questioning of the roles and behaviour imposed on women by the male psyche. The more accessible short feature *Sonia* (NFB, 1986) is a sensitive study of an artist/professor who develops Alzheimer's disease and of her relationship with her daughter Roxanne as the disease takes its course.

THE POST-REFERENDUM GENERATION IN QUEBEC CINEMA

Quebec film-makers who began their feature careers in the eighties found a climate less favourable to experimentation and protest than that of the sixties and seventies. The nationalistic flavour disappeared as independence was put 'on the back burner', first by the 1980 referendum and then by the Parti Québécois. More women began making films, but their works were rarely influenced by the critical feminist documentary; instead, they were striving to normalize women's participation in the film-making profession and their works often showed women in positive central roles.

Louise Carré, after a long career at the NFB, founded *La Maison des Quatre* with Denyse Benoit and André Théberge in 1977. Their first film was *Ça peut pas être l'hiver, on n'a même pas eu d'été* (1980), in which a younger version of Brecht's Unworthy Old Woman gradually adjusts to widowhood and builds a new life for herself over the objections of her family. *Qui a tiré sur nos histoires d'amour?* (1986) presented another woman making it on her own as a middle-aged radio talk-show host in Sorel who attempts to squeeze in a bit of social comment from time to time. **Danièle Suissa** has directed comparable work in her films for TV, such as *Kate Morris, Vice-President* (1983, CBC's 'For the Record'), and *Rose Café* (1986), about a woman fighting against male betrayal to succeed as a restaurant owner. **Micheline Lanctôt** was a film animator before her acting career got under way with *La vraie nature de Bernadette*. Her own films have provoked comparisons with Woody Allen, Robert Bresson, Lina Wertmuller, and recent French comedies. *L'homme à tout faire* (1980), her homage to the low-key wit and human warmth of the Czech movies of the sixties, followed the travels of a somewhat tentative young handyman with a weakness for the ladies, who always seem to take amorous advantage of him. *Sonatine* (1983) is a three-part story of two adolescent girls discovering life in Montreal, one with a bus-driver whose route she always takes (until he's transferred), the other with a Bulgarian sailor as a stowaway (until he turns her in); in the third part the two disappointed girls get together and vainly challenge the world to prevent their suicide.

The Swiss-born **Léa Pool**'s experimental *Strass Café* (1980) owed more to the French art-house style of Alain Resnais, Jean Cayrol, and Marguerite Duras, than any other film made here. Disembodied voices, recounting fragments of the lives of two enigmatic nightclub performers, are heard over extended stills of urban landscapes. *La femme de l'hôtel* (ACPAV, 1984) is, in Pool's words, a study of 'rootlessness, not belonging and internal exile'. Three women in Montreal—Andréa, a film-maker suffering from writer's block about her latest protagonist, a nameless actress destined for the part, and a mysterious disturbed outsider called Estelle—drift together as Estelle, the woman in the hotel, comes to obsess Andréa as a possible model for her character; as the film evolves, the identities of the three women begin to coalesce. In *Anne Trister* (1985) fragmentation, exile, artistic obsession, and feminine identity are interwoven in the story of a young woman who cannot win comfort from her mother at her father's premature death in Israel, and heads for Montreal, where she embarks on a journey of self-recovery, through her work as an artist and in a liberating relationship with an older woman. In her three works, Pool has moved from the obscure to the more accessible, a trajectory that may coincide with growing artistic confidence and a reconciliation with the rootlessness of the immigrant.

Yves Simoneau has made a number of stylish films for a broader audience, including two crime-thrillers starring Pierre Curzi and Marie Tufo: *Les yeux rouges* (1982), and the more widely-seen *Pouvoir intime / Blind Trust* (1983), the story of a botched hold-up and political corruption. *Pourquoi l'étrange Monsieur Zolock s'intéressait-il tant à la bande dessinée?* (1982) was a composite film, using a detective story as a frame for alternating interviews with comic strip writers and animated sequences of their work. *Les fous de Bassan / In the Shadow of the Wind* (1986) adapted Anne Hébert's novel, a dark tale of sexual desire and repression based on a night in 1936 that shattered the closed Protestant fishing community of Griffin Creek in the Gaspé.

Jean-Claude Lauzon has declared his debt to the eccentric underground world of André Forcier's films and yet his first feature *Un zoo la nuit* (1987) is equally reminiscent of Beneix (*Diva*) or the new British Channel 4 New Wave films for its combination of sordid violence and moments of sentiment in a story about an ex-convict's efforts to keep the drug-deal proceeds he had hidden before being caught.

REGIONAL FRANCOPHONE CINEMA—QUEBEC AND BEYOND

The best examples of French-language regional cinema inside Quebec are **André Blanchard**'s short feature *Beat* (1975) and the longer *L'Hiver bleu* (1978). Both films were shot around Rouyn-Noranda in Abitibi and offer a positive regional counterbalance to Noël's *Ti-cul Tougas*. They show young people seeking solutions to their sense of isolation and marginalization in an economically depressed community. Each film dwells on a contrasted pair of girls, an introvert longing for escape and an extrovert seeking to involve herself in collective activities in the community.

Beyond Quebec, francophone cinema has flourished best in New Brunswick, where the NFB had a regional French studio. **Léonard Forest** was one of the pioneers of Acadian film, but his films were primarily documentary. **Anna Girouard**'s short feature *Abandounée* (1976) dramatized the tribulations of an Acadian family in Sainte-Marie N.B. during the Depression. **Claude Renaud**'s shorts *La Confession* (1977) and *Souvenir d'un écolier* (1978) situated their action in the two bastions of minority French language beyond Quebec, Church and school. *Massabielle* (Jacques Savoie, 1983) is a short resettlement drama comparable to others made in Abitibi and Gaspésie within Quebec. *De l'autre côté de la glace* (Serge Morin & Georges Dufaux, 1983) uses a hockey game between the locals and a Canadian team as a symbolic setting for Acadian aspirations. *La Sagouine* (Jean-Paul Fugère, 1976–77), a series of seven sketches for Radio-Canada taken from Antonine Maillet's stage-play for a single voice, may be canned theatre but it preserves Viola Léger's memorable performance as the canny old woman representing the spirit of the region.

The best fictional work to come out of the NFB's French production in Winnipeg is **Claude Grenier**'s *Le vieillard et l'enfant* (1985). Adapted from a story in Gabrielle Roy's *La Route d'Altamont*, it is a sensitive, lyrical study of a trip to Lake Winnipeg, the last for an old man (Jean Duceppe) and the magical first for a young girl.

From francophone Ontario comes **Jacques Ménard**'s *Rien qu'en passant* (1976), a short-feature that rather didactically dramatizes the linguistic assimilation of Franco-Ontarian youth and **Michel Macina**'s short *Métallo Blues* (1985) starring Gabriel Arcand as a northern steelworker who loses his job and retreats to the country with his guitar and his girl-friend.

CHILDREN'S FILM IN QUEBEC

Apart from the NFB's dated Ti-Jean short stories from the fifties, and Roger Laliberté's independently-made 16mm adventure features (from 1956 to 1965) that recall the Belgian comic-book tradition of Tintin and company, a tradition of films for children has been slow to develop in Quebec. **Bernard Gosselin**'s *Le martien de Noël* (1970) was a Christmas formula-film that offered a parable on the need for tolerance and understanding by showing the conspiratorial friendship between children and an exotic visitor. **Richard Lavoie**, an independent documentarist, made two films for children in 1973, *La cabane* and the feature *Guitare*. Both were shot in an observational non-interventionist style in the natural surroundings near his home in Tewkesbury, just north of Quebec City, and both succeeded in conveying a magical sense of children's adventure (at a backwoods cabin or on an island) without resorting to special effects or high drama. The first was shot with his own children, and in the second the children were given full liberty to construct their own script. The NFB 'Toulmonde parle français' (1974) included four live-action short films for children, three of them written and directed by **André Melançon**, the best maker of children's films in Canada to-day. His reputation in English Canada came with the immensely successful *La Guerre des tuques / The Dog Who Stopped the War* (1984), the first of producer Rock Demers' eight-film series 'Contes pout Tous / Tales for All'. Two teams of school-children in the snowy landscape of Charlevoix County do battle around a magical, gadget-filled fort, until the accidental death of one team's dog brings an end to the conflict. After writing the French version of Rubbo's *Peanut Butter Solution*, Melançon directed *Bach et Bottine* (1986), the story of an orphan with a menagerie of pets—including a skunk called Bottine—who goes to live with an uncle absorbed by his preparations for a Bach concert.

With their magical transformations of both the natural and the urban world, and what André Breton would call their rejection of the fantastic in favour of the marvellous, Quebec's films for children are close to the local traditions we have observed in the sixties films of Jutra and company.

5

FICTIONAL FILM IN ENGLISH SINCE 1939

GOVERNMENT POLICY AND THE CANADIAN FILM INDUSTRY

After the war the possibility of launching an English-Canadian feature film industry was again raised publicly. The success of the National Film Board and the coming of radio drama in English—Andrew Allan's weekly 'Stage' series began in 1944—suggested that a talent pool comparable to Quebec's might emerge. But the Mackenzie King government was more interested in reducing the severe trade deficit with the U.S. that had accompanied postwar reconstruction. In 1947, the year following the first package of import restrictions, Hollywood had repatriated a profit of 17 million dollars from Canada. Ross McLean, the Film Commissioner, was calling for compulsory re-investment of a portion of Canadian box-office profits into Canadian production and guaranteed American distribution of Canadian shorts. The American movie moguls moved quickly, and within months they had secured government agreement for the Canadian Co-operation Project. To help close the dollar gap Hollywood promised to promote American tourist traffic to Canada by increasing the use of Canadian locations, improving Canadian investment opportunities in American film production, and opening US markets to Canadian films. Most of this was window dressing; the chief outcome was the appointment of a Canadian liaison officer in Hollywood who reviewed scripts with a view to inserting references to Canada. The Project, which lasted for about ten years, successfully killed hopes of a Canadian film industry during that time.

Twenty-two English-language features, however, were produced and released in Canada from war's end to 1962, of which eight date from the CCP decade. These were mainly low-budget second-feature quickies, some shot in studios built for the short-lived Quebec feature boom, others in and around Toronto: *Bush Pilot* (**Sterling Campbell**, 1946), a romantic action drama; *Oedipus Rex* (**Tyrone Guthrie**, 1956), a film of a Guthrie stage production from the early years of Ontario's Stratford Festival; and *Now That April's Here* (**William Davidson**, 1958), which adapted four Morley Callaghan stories. One TV writer from Toronto, **Sidney J. Furie**, directed two minor teenage-rebellion films there on his way to a career in Britain and Hollywood. *Forbidden Journey* (**Richard Jarvis & Cecil Maiden**, 1949), a slow-paced Cold War thriller, was shot in Montreal and starred a young Jan Rubes. James Clavell made his first film in Vancouver, *The Sweet and the Bitter* (1962), set in the aftermath of the war-time internment of Japanese Canadians.

By 1963 the NFB had already produced six French-language features in the 'Panoramique' series. That year saw its first English-language feature, also originally planned for TV, *The Drylanders* (**Don Haldane**, 1963), a Saskatchewan family saga—from the hardships of settlement in 1907 through the twenties' boom and the thirties' dustbowl to drought's end. The dramatic structure, which recalls that of the old CGMPB's *Heritage* (1939), affirmed the pioneers' will to master Nature through community rather than through the rugged individualism of the American Western.

In the ten years following *The Drylanders*, as the Quebec New Wave flourished, English-language features in Canada were still few and far between. The establishment of the Canadian Film Development Corporation (CFDC) in 1967 was the first of a series of government initiatives designed to stimulate a feature film industry. In two respects it was the converse of previous government interventions. It encouraged theatrical features rather than short informative films, and, whereas the NFB and CBC-TV had cultural missions to perform, the CFDC was commercial in outlook, assessing the profitability of projects from scripts, providing production and distribution assistance, and monitoring the business practices of the producing company. To avoid the mistakes of the thirties' quota system, Canadian distribution guarantees were expected and Canadian content was required (quotas of Canadians as major participants), although international co-productions could be included. But this did not lead to a vibrant new film culture in English Canada. The emphasis on scripts tended to play down the improvisational style inspired by living documentary. Because of commercial pressures popular genres were favoured over projects that did not fit the programming priorities of American-based theatre chains. But CFDC help did reach English-language features welcomed as 'distinctively Canadian'—illustrative and constructive of Canadian culture.

In 1974 the federal government added tax incentives to accelerate the privatization of feature film financing. The Capital Cost Allowance program allowed Canadian film investments to be used as a 100 per cent tax shelter, which reduced the risks of speculation and occasioned a boom in film production; but it also reduced the regulatory role of the CFDC. Although the boom provided new outlets for private producers and the promise of experience for film crews in the major centres, it also attracted promoters and profiteers with promises of upfront cash without the quality controls and distribution guarantees the CFDC had sought. The boom petered out in the 1980s and the program is now being wound down.

In July 1983 the CFDC began its Broadcast Fund and effectively broadened its mandate to include video and film production for TV (it subsequently adopted the name Telefilm Canada). Two varieties of production were given a boost by this change. One was the short drama to fit a 30- or 60-minute TV slot; the other was dual production—films aimed at both TV and theatrical markets, but cut into different versions: the theatrical feature (90-150 mins) and the longer TV mini-series (several episodes filling fixed time-slots).

The pool of talent for the infant industry came principally from three sources: the documentarists of the NFB or the CBC, early TV drama at the CBC, and the new university film boards. These various groupings—often sharing resources and crews—that began making features in the sixties were not 'schools' in the art-history sense; they were looser than that, and their initial élan was often lost. Their films were subjected to the demands of a commercial cinema for a mass audience conditioned by the techniques and conventions appropriated and promoted by Hollywood. Tolerance for the idiosyncratic and the tentative was limited; one box-office failure could bring a promising career in features to an end. Accordingly, many of the film-makers in each group reached for the mass market—pursuing international (American or British) careers as many Canadians had done before them, opting for Canadian-made exploitation films (formula-films targeting mass audiences), or moving (back) into the greater security of television drama.

DOCUMENTARY STYLES AND SOCIAL MISSIONS

The English documentarists who turned to dramatic features in the sixties adopted an observational shooting style (with the new light equipment), open-ended structures, contemporary social settings and themes, and archival footage in film dramas either improvised (or researched) from a critical personal experience or dramatized as case-histories of social problems. Most of the first generation were Montrealers or Torontonians, often in their thirties, and their films usually concentrate on those two cities.

The tensions that generated dramatic conflict in their films were not rooted in a sense of emerging national identity as were those in Quebec films of the time, but were found in the disaffection of contemporary youth in a conflict of generations that had a more international flavour. Don Owen, Ron Kelly, and George Kaczender all made films about rebellious teenagers in middle-class families. **Don Owen's** *Nobody Waved Goodbye* is usually singled out as the groundbreaker. Like the first features by Groulx and Carle, it grew from a short (on juvenile delinquency). In Owen's loose script, Peter rebels against his suburban Toronto family and, following a series of misdemeanours, abandons his pregnant girl-friend Julie and flees the city in a stolen car. Twenty years later, with *Unfinished Business* (1984), Owen returned to Peter and Julie, now divorced and middle-aged, and confronting their own teenage daughter's coming-of-age pains, but the fresh improvised style of the former film was lost. Owen's unfinished trilogy, consisting of the short feature *Notes for a Film About Donna and Gail* (1966) and the feature *The Ernie Game* (NFB/CBC, 1967, 2 **CFA**s), were characterized as portrayals of the psychedelic generation, and have evoked comparisons with Jean-Luc Godard and Jack Kerouac. *Donna and Gail* introduced us to the two girls who, in *The Ernie Game*, become contrasting poles of attraction for the marginal Ernie, a recently released schizophrenic who drifts into delinquency and thoughts of suicide. *Donna and Gail* experimented with different framing devices for the action—on-screen and off-screen voice, interviews, staged action and observed action—while *The Ernie Game* played with colour in its presentation of the drifter's psychotic personality. Following a number of dramatized case-histories of disaffected youth—notably the award-winning short *Phoebe* (1964), on teen-age pregnancy—**George Kaczender**'s *Don't Let the Angels Fall*, the first official Canadian entry at Cannes, portrays a family in which two sons rebel as the father engages in a short affair before returning to a cold marriage: one runs away from home, the other is arrested in a student demonstration. Kaczender's subsequent fiction films have aimed for the commercial market: *U-Turn* (1973), about a successful man who drops everything to seek out a woman in blue he had once seen on a ferry; *In Praise of Older Women* (1977), the erotic coming of age of a Hungarian student who escapes the 1958 uprising and comes to Canada; and *Agency* (1979), a suspense thriller on the theme of subliminal advertising.

The flavour of the broader social rebellion of sixties' youth came through most strongly in **Robin Spry**'s films: his documentary *Flowers on a One-Way Street* (1967) depicted confrontations between Toronto hippies and City Hall, and the feature *Prologue* (NFB, 1969) showed a Montreal couple parting company to act out the two extreme forms of response (as in *Don't Let the Angels Fall*)—active protest (Jesse joins the demonstrations outside the Democratic National Convention in Chicago) and utopian withdrawal (Karen joins a rural commune)—before rejecting these other worlds and reuniting. Gilles Marsolais considered this film the perfect marriage of fiction and the direct style, although others felt the introduction of sixties' counterculture celebrities and the trip to Chicago sat awkwardly in the plot. **Mort Ransen**, after documentary shorts on school drop-outs and a drug treatment centre, went further than Spry with *Christopher's Movie Matinee* (1968), which defies generic classification and anticipates Jutra's *Wow* (1969) by showing a group of teenagers making a film about their desire for social change: they act out real and imaginary events until the escalation of confrontational politics caused the NFB to call back their film crew, a reminder of the force of the 'general sanction'. Ransen's recent *Bayo* (NFB/CBC, 1985) made use of Georges Dufaux's lyrical photography to combine scenes of life in a Newfoundland outport with a young boy's perception of the fantasies of his grandfather, who is unwilling to leave the ocean, and of his mother, who is anxious to make a new start in Toronto.

With the new social consciousness implied by the NFB's 'Challenge for Change', social realism emerged in the dramatic feature with an emphasis on working-class characters and the marginal underside of inner cities. Foremost was **Don Shebib**'s *Goin' Down the Road* (1970), which collected three **CFA**s, including Best Feature. Like *Nobody Waved Goodbye*, it grew from a shorter documentary (about Maritimers moving to Toronto) and retained Shebib's interest in the urban subcultures of his earlier work at the CBC and the NFB. The shooting style of Richard Leiterman, who had much experience in the living documentary style, combined with Shebib's editing of sequences to accentuate the rhythms and forms of real places. Convincingly acted from William Fruet's spare script, the film plots the cycle of Pete and Joey, two Maritimers in Toronto, from marginal vagabondage to an attempt to settle down to work and domestic life, and back to marginal vagabondage. For them Toronto is the place false dreams are made of; as their toehold on security fades into criminality and flight, their dream-journey concludes with defeat in the face of social and material forces beyond their control or comprehension. After *Rip-Off* (1971), which reverses the doomed dream-journey—four middle-class high-school boys in a rock band leave the city to found a commune on country property inherited by one of them—Shebib made *Between Friends* (1973), in which the hopes for escape lie in the planned heist of a northern mining company's payroll. The interaction of marginal characters who come together is intricately and ironically developed before their dreams are thwarted, with deadly consequences. *Second Wind* (1976) substituted the idea of a different life and community for its central character (competitive running instead of the corporate world of the stockbroker) for the dream-journey of a central couple or group. After *Fish Hawk* (1979), a family entertainment feature, Shebib returned to social realism with *Heartaches* (1981), about the vicissitudes of life for two working-class girl-friends who enjoy a temporary friendship in Toronto before returning to former boy-friends. In all his films, whether they portray working-class characters or not, Shebib combines the foiled dreams of escape from social reality with the tensions and pressures of flawed male-female relationships.

After writing a number of scripts, including those for Shebib's first two features, **William Fruet** wrote and directed *Wedding in White* (1972). This brilliantly-acted adaptation of his own stage-play owes little to the documentary-film tradition, but shares with it a relentless naturalism in its bleak portrayal of the claustrophobic lives of a small-town family during the Second World War; the family is dominated by the men (principally Donald Pleasence) whose bad faith, self-delusion, and ignorance lead to the victimization of the timid teenage daughter Jeannie (Carol Kane).

Peter Pearson's *The Best Damn Fiddler from Calabogie to Kaladar* (NFB, 1969, 8 **CFA**s) combined a case-history of a family living on the poverty line in Eastern Ontario's bushland with a dramatic story-line that brought the eldest daughter (Margot Kidder) into focus as she eventually decides she must leave to find a better life. *Paperback Hero* (1973), which is more schematic than *The Rowdyman* with which it is often compared, combines the fantasy-world of the protagonist (Keir Dullea), who adopts the persona and trappings of a tough Western gunslinger, and the reality of small-town Saskatchewan with its depressed economy and small-time ice-hockey team.

Paul Lynch, who came from Britain and made many documentaries for the CBC in the sixties and seventies before beginning a partnership with writers Bill Gray and John Hunter, made two films along the lines of Pearson's portrayal of losers in small town Ontario: *The Hard Part Begins* (1973), about a small-time country singer, Jim King, who returns to his home town and suffers a series of humiliations and disappointments; and *Blood and Guts* (1977), innovatively shot by a young Mark Irwin, which substituted a wrestling road show for country singing. But with *Prom Night* (1979), a tale of a mad murderer on the loose at a high-school prom, Lynch abandoned southern Ontario for Ohio, choosing the 'Proctor and Gamble method of making movies' (Lynch's term) and a splatter-film for the youth market. He used this formula—derived from *Hallowe'en* and *Texas Chainsaw Massacre*—again in *Humongous* (1981), with a northwoods setting. His *Cross-Country* (1982) was a crime thriller that managed to disguise its Montreal locations as various American cities.

The working-class social realism of *Goin' Down the Road* was pursued further by **Clay Borris**, who began with a series of short dramatizations about his own family that exemplified New Brunswick migrants' experience of survival in Toronto's Cabbagetown: in particular, the much admired *Rose's House* ('Challenge for Change', NFB,1977). His first feature, *Alligator Shoes* (1980), was a more developed story of two brothers and their relations with a mentally unstable young aunt who comes to stay with them. These films realized the synthesis of direct cinema and personal statement in a dramatic format that is central to a contemporary trend in both Canadian film and theatre. But although *Alligator Shoes* won a prize at the Mannheim festival and was shown at Cannes, few Canadians will have seen it, unless they caught its airing on CBC-TV.

A different marriage of dramatic and documentary elements occurred in *Warrendale* (1967), *A Married Couple* (1969), and *Come On Children* (1972). All directed by **Allan King** in Toronto, these were not dramatic features, although the first two gained the theatrical release and reception usually reserved for such films. Documentaries shot in the direct 'living-cinema' style by the same teams King worked with in Vancouver and London, they show groups of people under stress, viewed intimately without apparent intervention, and edited to form a dramatic shape similar to the films discussed above—King calls them 'dramatic structures'. In *Warrendale* the film-makers lived for a time in a group home for emotionally disturbed children; in *A Married Couple* with an urban middle-class family undergoing a marital crisis; and in *Come On Children* with a group of disaffected youngsters who leave the city for a farm. These enclosed worlds, presented with voyeuristic intensity, allow for considerable ambiguity in the interplay between authentic, self-generated behaviour and histrionic performance mediated by a sense of spectacle. They show similarities with the later *Who's in Charge ?* (1983), the record of a four-day meeting between 28 unemployed Canadians and a number of consultants and counsellors in an exploration of unemployed people's feelings about their experience. King's films have sparked controversy about the implications of making a spectacle of the distress and anger of the powerless for the pleasure and entertainment of the viewing public—a curious reaction, since such subject-matter has not only been at the heart of much of the living documentary tradition but provides a human dimension to an otherwise intellectual problem. King's greatest success in more conventional feature films has been *Who Has Seen the Wind* (1977) from W.O. Mitchell's novel of the Depression in the Prairies as seen through the eyes of a young boy.

Silence of the North (1981) was a less succesful drama starring Ellen Burstyn as a pioneering woman in the Arctic. King has also directed numerous adaptations of plays and short stories for TV, as well as the compilational video *Six War Years* (1975), from Barry Broadfoot's oral history of Canadian Second World War experiences.

Murray Markowitz also made two living documentaries in the King style—*More Than One* (1971), about three retarded people, and *August and July* (1973), about a lesbian couple—but, like Michel Moreau (see Chapter 3), he was more willing to intervene to structure the scenes. Markowitz is better known for his highly dramatic adaptations of two controversial Canadian murder trials in which guilty verdicts were subsequently questioned: *Recommendation for Mercy* (1975), on the 14-year-old Stephen Truscott trial of 1959, and *I Miss You, Hugs and Kisses* (1978), on the Peter Demeter trial of 1974.

As in the features of French-Canadian documentarists, news reporters occasionally became protagonists in the English-language films. On the lighter side, *Why Rock the Boat?* (NFB, 1974), adapted from William Weintraub's satirical novel set in the Montreal of the forties, was directed by veteran NFB documentarist **John Howe**, while *One Man* (**Robin Spry**, NFB, 1977) featured Len Cariou as an investigative reporter who stumbles upon a pollution scandal.

Although justice cannot be done to TV films here, mention must be made of the CBC's series of journalistic dramas, 'For the Record'. The series was in large measure inspired by John Hirsch's emphasis on TV's social mission, following his arrival as head of TV drama in 1974. Directors for the series that began in 1976 under Ralph L. Thomas included many of Canada's prominent film-makers: Carle, Jutra, Mankiewicz, Danièle Suissa from French Quebec; Almond, Brittain, Dalen, Fruet, Haldane, King, Pinsent, Shebib, Spry, Trent, Walker, Waxman, and Anne Wheeler from English Canada. Its best early works were political dramas of recent events that portrayed recognizable personalities. Pearson's most notable contributions were *The Insurance Man from Ingersoll* (1976), on political corruption in Ontario, and *The Tar Sands* (1977), on the Athabasca Tar Sands negotiations in Alberta, a docudrama that earned the CBC a lawsuit from Premier Peter Lougheed. Later, the films dwelt more on social issues: Allan King worked from Rick Salutin's play *Maria* (1977), about an Italian-Canadian's efforts to unionize her factory; Donald

Brittain made *Running Man* (1981), about the anguish of a married high-school teacher who becomes aware of his homosexuality; Gordon Pinsent directed *A Far Cry from Home* (1981), the most widely distributed of the series, which followed a battered wife's struggle for escape. Outside the series, **Ralph L. Thomas** produced Robin Spry's docudrama *Drying Up the Streets* (1978), using direct cinema style sequences of life on Toronto's streets to follow an ex-addict (Don Francks) who embarks on a quest to find his daughter while breaking up a drug racket. Thomas directed *Ticket to Heaven* (1983), set in the world of religious cults, and *The Terry Fox Story* (1983, **CFA** for Best Feature), which enacted the private dramas behind the one-legged athlete's cross-Canada run attempt to raise funds for cancer research.

A new synthesis of documentary and drama has come from the NFB's Studio B, and its Alternative Drama Program. **Giles Walker**, **John N. Smith**, and **David Wilson** have worked on five features, beginning with a rather unpromising experiment, *The Masculine Mystique* (Walker & Smith, 1984), in which four men (NFB employees) discuss their difficulties in coping with sexual relations in the light of women's emancipation—a rather self-indulgent, personal document intercut with dramatizations of their embarrassments. Two of the improvised characters were featured in the highly successful comedy *90 Days* (Walker, 1985), in which one tries for a mail-order bride from Korea and the other, Alex, is given an opportunity to enter the sperm-donor business. *The Last Straw* (Walker, 1987) pursues Alex to world fame, fortune, and downfall. **John N. Smith**, on the other hand, has returned to the roots of the NFB's documentary/drama fusion with *Sitting in Limbo* (1986), filmed among the Caribbean youth of Montreal with a script based on community interviews and research. While its tale of teenage pregnancy, unemployment, and racism borders on moral didacticism and stereotyping at times, it has the verve and wit that often accompany the observational style. *Train of Dreams* (1978) centres on juvenile delinquency.

The documentarists' dramatic works seldom show the attention given by Quebec films of the sixties to social and cultural identity. Spry, whose feature documentary *Action* (1970) and its short-feature sequel *Reaction* (1973) constitute the best English-language analyses of the events of the 1970 October Crisis and its aftermath, made two attempts to cope with the bi-national identity: the short feature *Don't*

Forget 'Je me souviens' (1979), about the stresses on a French-English marriage after a transfer from Montreal to Toronto, and *Suzanne* (1980), a loose adaptation of Ronald Sutherland's novel *Snow lark* (1971), in which the conflicting values of the two Canadian solitudes are symbolized in Suzanne, the child of a mixed marriage. As for Canada-U.S. relations, Owen's *Partners* (1976) explored patterns of partnership and their dissolution within a crime romance that offers a parallel between male-female relations and international business relations.

The work of the ex-documentarists has traditionally been seen by film scholars as the defining genius of English-Canadian film. So strong is the tradition they represent and the continuities that can be established between them and the various strands of NFB/CBC documentary that critics frequently attribute their characteristics to film-makers schooled in other Canadian cultural traditions. When these links cannot readily be made, critics are sometimes reluctant to accord Canadian status to the works of such film-makers.

QUALITY DRAMA

One such group consists of the directors who worked in the CBC Toronto drama department in the fifties and sixties. **Paul Almond** directed over one hundred CBC dramas before becoming the most widely-heralded new Canadian film director of the late sixties. **Harvey Hart** also broke into theatrical features during this period. **Norman Jewison** left Canada for a distinguished film career in the U.S.A. with such films as *The Cincinnati Kid* (1965), *In the Heat of the Night* (1967), and, most recently, *A Soldier's Story* (1984) and *Agnes of God* (1985). **Sydney Newman**, who had begun in the NFB, worked in the same CBC unit as Almond, Hart, and Jewison and, after a spell in England as a TV drama head, returned to become Film Commissioner in the midst of the censorship controversy in the early seventies. **Ted Kotcheff**, after starting as a stage-hand at CBC TV, worked with Newman both there and in England. In addition to a career in Britain, Australia, and Hollywood, he has returned twice to Canada to make film adaptations of Mordecai Richler's novels. **Silvio Narrizzano** left in 1956 and worked mainly in British TV, returning in the seventies for one important Canadian feature. Later graduates from CBC-TV drama were British immigrants **Eric Till**, who also made features in Britain and the U.S., and the late **Peter Carter** who, besides making Crawley Film productions for the CBC, worked on films by Almond and Till.

On the whole, this was a slightly older group than the first generation of feature-makers from documentary backgrounds. They have a more 'international' image—their names appear in *Halliwell's Filmgoer's Companion*. They also attached more importance to directing actors and developing strong scripts—aspects initially played down by the documentarists. Where the relation of place to character was important in their films, it tended to be symbolic rather than naturalistic (a projection of mood or personality rather than a constraining force). Although Almond wrote the scripts of his own trilogy in the European auteurist tradition, most directors took on commissions or adaptations. The actors came from TV or theatre and the leads were often imports with box-office appeal.

The Almond-Bujold trilogy, *Isabel* (1968), *Act of the Heart* (1970), and *Journey* (1972), stirred considerable critical controversy. Those who viewed the fusion of fiction and documentary as the defining Canadian tradition found it histrionic and introverted. Those who saw the Hollywood drama as the 'only practical alternative' to the indigenous docudrama found it obscurantist and pretentious. But many may have been disappointed not to find further confirmation of a narrow view of the Canadian mainstream. **Paul Almond**'s trilogy is often likened to the films of Ingmar Bergman, more for its metaphysical exploration of madness than for common structural or stylistic features. It could have been influential in the genesis of the art film in Canada, had it not been for extremely negative reviews by critics such as Martin Knelman and Urjo Kareda. Each work shows a metaphorical attempt to build identity through quest and reconstruction. The central woman in each work—played by Geneviève Bujold, then married to Almond— embarks on a period of self-doubt and struggles to rebuild a sense of selfhood. In *Isabel* the crisis comes in the days following the death of Isabel's mother at the family farmstead on the Gaspé coast; images of her family's past of violence and incest return in many guises to haunt her, some rooted in reality, others produced by her own imagination. The repressed sexuality associated with family in *Isabel* is identified with spiritual belief and religious practice in *Act of the Heart*, which traces the shifting relationship between a governess and an Augustinian monk (Donald Sutherland). In the more poetic and figurative *Journey* a woman's visit to a dreamlike pioneering community from another time on the Saguenay River represents her efforts to recover from personal catastrophe. After *Journey'* s commercial failure, Almond returned to scriptwriting and TV. In recent years he has re-emerged to make *Ups and Downs* (1983), a modest drama set in a boarding-school, about the trials of growing up in an isolated setting. Made with a cast of students from the private-school in Victoria B.C. where it was shot, the film was a 'quality drama' rejoinder to the adolescent gross-outs of Hollywood and its Canadian clones.

These tormented inner searches for psychic liberation are rare in other films by the first CBC group. **Harvey Hart** returned to Canada from Hollywood for the co-production *Fortune and Men's Eyes* (1971), from John Herbert's stage-play about the progressive brutali-zation of a young man experiencing jail for the first time. Brought in to replace an American director amid charges of sensationalism, Hart, who had adapted Brendan Behan's *The Quare Fellow* for TV in 1967, failed to satisfy those who wanted greater documentary realism and sense of place (despite the use of a former prison in Quebec); he accorded more importance to the dramatic interplay between the actors, heightened by the attentive cinematography of Georges Dufaux, who, in addition to his documentary experience, had shot Almond's *Isabel*. With *The Pyx* (1973), Hart made a slick crime thriller starring Christopher Plummer (his first Canadian film) and Karen Black, filmed in the more natural, fluid style of René Verzier, whose work was already well-known from his films with Carle and Denis Héroux. Despite its identifiable Montreal setting and its use of well-known Quebec actors, the film confirmed Hart's preference for the 'inter-national style'. Returning again for *Goldenrod* in 1976, he won a **CFA** for best direction in a sentimental redemption story about an Albertan bronco-buster fighting back from the brink of suicide after a serious accident and the break-up of his marriage. Hart, whose more recent Canadian films have not gained the same recognition, has continued in American TV.

Eleven years separate **Ted Kotcheff**'s two films adapted from nov-els by Mordecai Richler, *The Apprenticeship of Duddy Kravitz* (1974) and *Joshua Then and Now* (1985). Both films, which won various **CFA**s and did well on the international festival circuit—especially *Duddy Kravitz*—demonstrate characteristics of the 'international style' in Canada. Shot in and around many of Richler's own haunts in Montreal's Jewish ghetto and beyond to upper-class Westmount and the rural playgrounds of Montreal's wealthy, they do not stint on Canadian locations. But, like the novels that Richler adapted to the screen, their chronicling of their hero's climb out of the ghetto through a series of hilarious adventures, compromised friendships, and moral sacrifices embodies more universal values. Imported actors take top roles—a lively and equivocal Duddy played by Richard Dreyfuss early in his career. *Joshua Then and Now* is less successful, perhaps because of its dual form (four hours for a TV mini-series, shorter for theatrical release) and the greater complexity of its source. The distance separating the international style from the 'indigenous' tradition may best be seen in *The Apprenticeship of Duddy Kravitz*, where Duddy's foray into the movie world with a drunken film director to make a pretentious and disastrous documentary for an elaborate bar mitzvah can be seen as a hilarious spoof of the excesses implicit in the NFB's Griersonian tradition.

Eric Till's theatrical films—*A Great Big Thing* (1966), about a day in the life of a Montreal drifter who has been compared to Don Owen's Ernie; *A Fan's Notes* (1970), a study, based on Fred Exley's 1968 novel, of the compulsively vicarious world of the sports fan; and *If You Could See What I Hear* (1982), a story about a blind student that mixed elements of campus farce with moral uplift—have never lived up to the standard of his TV work. He returned to TV in the seventies with *The National Dream* (1974), *The Newcomers* (1976–78), and *Home Fires* (1983). **Silvio Narizzano**'s *Why Shoot the Teacher* (1977), starring Bud Cort and Samantha Eggar, was adapted from Max Braithwaite's novel about a young teacher from the East who takes his first job in a one-room schoolhouse on the Prairies during the Depression. **Peter Carter**'s *The Rowdyman* (1971) relied heavily on the Newfoundland roots of its writer and star Gordon Pinsent in the role of the rebellious Will Cole who refuses to take life seriously until it begins to hit him back hard, although its major supporting actors (Frank Converse and Will Gere) were imports. Carter's later works were Hollywood North action dramas, such as *High-Ballin'* (1978), a trucking version of *Shane* complete with a hero called Rane, played by Peter Fonda.

Despite the drift toward formula films, the spirit of the quality drama can be found in two films directed by Canadian immigrants in the seventies. *Lies My Father Told Me* (1975) by **Jan Kadar**—best known for his Czech film *The Shop on Main Street* (1965)—was the story of a family of first-generation Russian Jewish immigrants set in the Montreal of the twenties. Despite three years of production delays and problems, this sentimental, nostalgic light comedy won 5 **CFAs** and a Golden Globe from the Hollywood critics. The American **Richard Benner** worked two years as a story-editor at the CBC before directing *Outrageous !* (1977), an adaptation of Margaret Gibson's short story 'Making It' from the collection *The Butterfly Ward* (1976) that co-incided with Jutra's adaptation of her 'Ada' for CBC's 'For the Record'. The semi-autobiographical story of the friendship between a schizophrenic (Hollis McLaren) and a gay hairdresser turned female impersonator (Craig Russell) owed much of its appeal to Russell's bravura stage performances. Benner then spent ten years in New York before returning for the sequel *Too Outrageous* (1987).

Among recent TV directors **Martin Lavut** is most notable for *Charlie Grant's War* (1984), from Anna Sandor's script, which featured a brilliant R.H. Thomson in a docudrama about a Canadian businessman in Austria who helped save 600 Jews from the Nazis, and *The Marriage Bed* (1986), Anna Sandor's adaptation of Constance Beresford-Howe's novel of 1981, the third in her trilogy of novels about modern women challenging contemporary wisdoms about their roles in society. **Kevin Sullivan** adapted *The Wild Pony* (1983) for pay-TV from Walt Morey's classic, and, from Lucy Maud Montgomery's children's classic, the blockbuster mini-series *Anne of Green Gables* and its sequel (1985–86), which owed much to Megan Follows' superlative Anne.

UP FROM THE UNIVERSITY UNDERGROUND

In the sixties the university underground offered a milieu for unconventional low-budget films and a ready-made parallel distribution circuit for first films. The underground film of the period often distinguished itself from the mainstream by breaking sexual taboos and ran afoul of provincial Censor Boards. Film-makers in this tradition did not serve an apprenticeship with either the NFB or the CBC. They were not particularly shaped by contemporary trends in documentary, and sought to make low-budget features as their *first* works. The centres of this activity in the mid- and late sixties were Toronto and Vancouver, although English-language directors also emerged from Montreal and Hamilton, Ont.

The University of Toronto sixties group consisted chiefly of David Secter, Iain Ewing, Clarke Mackey, and David Cronenberg, who worked on a number of projects together, *Winter Kept Us Warm* (1965), directed by **David Secter**, won a place on the international festival circuit with a story of a short but intense friendship between two male students that was particularly successful in conveying the atmosphere of campus life at the time. In **Iain Ewing**'s *Kill* (1968) Ewing plays himself in an Oedipal fantasy in which he and two other students plan to kill his father. **Clarke Mackey**'s *The Only Thing You Know* (1971, 2 **CFA**s), an episodic film about an 18-year-old co-ed student, adopted an improvisational acting style that bears comparison with the early films of Owen or Spry. The film received limited distribution and Mackey's subsequent career as a director, like Ewing's, has been marginal. Recent work includes *Taking Care*, an independent drama (with money from TVOntario) about mysterious deaths in a Toronto hospital that drew on public hearings held after a celebrated incident in 1985.

The most successful director to emerge from the U of T group is **David Cronenberg**. He shares with the university underground filmmakers a desire to attack taboos and to shatter complacencies. He began with two short features, *Stereo* (1969) and *Crimes of the Future* (1970), two science-fiction works that dwell on changes wrought upon the human mind by scientific intrusions: suppression of speech and an increase of telepathic capabilities in *Stereo*, and the sociosexual aftermath of a cosmetic-induced disease that has killed millions of women in *Crimes of the Future*. Little in the experimental visual and narrative style of these first films prepared audiences for the explosive effects of his commercial films. Known primarily for their ruthless depiction of visceral disintegration—the eruption of the inner body as it is organically transformed—Cronenberg's films have been subjected to both virulent attack and protracted academic discussion. They have been variously assimilated to the horror genre tradition: Robin Wood classifies them as 'reactionary' for apparently anathematizing the various forms of psycho-sexual liberation they posit; because they portray attempts to intervene in the natural order that go disastrously wrong, John Harkness identifies them with the science-fiction nightmare. Continuities with a recognizably Canadian sensibility have been sought: Cronenberg has described the moral ambivalence of his films (neither the status quo nor the desire to change it are unequivocally endorsed) as 'typically Canadian' inertia brought on by fear of the consequences of losing balance; Piers Handling argued that certain features—weak male characters, patterns of victimization, a distrust of technology—are among the constants of Canadian literature as outlined in Margaret Atwood's *Survival* and elaborated by such film critics as Bob Fothergill.

In *The Parasite Murders / Shivers* (1975) a mysterious parasite introduced by a scientist to correct bodily imbalances acts as a powerful aphrodisiac and deforming venereal disease. In *Rabid* (1976) plastic surgery on the main character (Marilyn Chambers) results in the growth of a blood-sucking underarm phallic spike that sets off a rabies-like plague. In *The Brood* (1979) patients of an experimental psychological clinic are urged to give bodily expression to their aggressions; this leads one separated wife and mother to give birth to a brood of murderous little monsters who begin killing her family members. In *Scanners* (1980) a drug called Ephemerol, administered to pregnant mothers as a tranquillizer, induces a telepathic condition called 'scanning' in their offspring, who form groups engaged in a violent struggle for power. In *Videodrome* (1982) a cable-TV businessman in Toronto picks up experimental TV satellite transmissions from Pittsburgh that show sado-masochistic fantasies and finds himself progressively taken over by them as the signal afflicts him with hallucination-causing brain tumours. In *The Fly* (1986), a substantial reworking of the 1958 minor American horror classic, a scientist triggers his own progressive metamorphosis into a monstrous fly. The distinctive visual style and atmosphere of Cronenberg's work derive in part from a group of collaborators sustained since 1978: Mark Irwin on camera, Carol Spier handling art direction, Ron Sanders editing, and Howard Shore contributing the music.

The group from McMaster University in Hamilton, Ont. included **John Hofsess**, **Peter Rowe**, and **Ivan Reitman**. Hofsess made two underground films inspired by the mood of sexual liberation—*The Palace of Pleasure* (1966), and *The Columbus of Sex*, (1969). The latter was judged obscene in an obscenity trial and copies were destroyed, but not before producers Reitman and Goldberg sold rights to an American company who added new footage and re-cut it for release as *My Secret Life*. **Peter Rowe**, who began film-making at McMaster with the experimental *Buffalo Airport Visions* (1967), won a **CFA** as most promising newcomer with *The Neon Palace* (1970), his personal tribute to the popular culture of the fifties and sixties. Rowe then worked in TV drama series and documentary before returning to theatrical production with his *Lost!* (1985), a dramatic re-enactment of a 1973 incident off the Pacific coast in which a sail-boat lost its bearings and overturned, bearing two brothers (Michael Hogan and Kenneth Walsh) and the pregnant wife of one of them (Helen Shaver). **Ivan Reitman** became the superstar of the group, noted for his irreverent, campy spoofs and comedies. His shorts at McMaster were followed by two cheap features—*Foxy Lady* and *Cannibal Girls*— before he began producing in Canada with Cronenberg's early features and Fruet's first horror film, and in the U.S. with *National Lampoon's Animal House* (Landis, 1978), which launched the adolescent gross-out comedies, of which his own *Meatballs* (1979), set in a summer camp, would establish a Canadian branch. He is now best known as the director of *Ghostbusters* (US, 1984), a sci-fi spoof starring Bill Murray; and *Legal Eagles* (US, 1986), starring Robert Redford.

From the University of British Columbia (U.B.C.) came the first films of Larry Kent in 1963, and of Jack Darcus in 1969. **Larry Kent**, who came to U.B.C. from South Africa, has directed sixteen features, including five for TV. He made the low-budget *The Bitter Ash* (1963) while a 29-year-old student at U.B.C. and, after his first three films, moved to Montreal. The sexual licence in *The Bitter Ash* caused campus screenings to be interrupted and earned the film a ban in Ontario. *High* (1967), which also included scenes of drug use, ran into difficulties with several provincial Boards of Censors. In 1984 his work was 'rediscovered' at the Toronto Festival of Festivals' retrospective of Canadian film and his early works, now in the National Film Archives, may return to circulation. His early films—*The Bitter*

Ash, *Sweet Substitute* (1964), *When Tomorrow Dies* (1965), and *Façade* (1968)—show people, trapped in unsatisfying relationships and alienated in their everyday life, seeking sexual release and a new identity elsewhere, but returning after a brief fling to their former partners. *High* (1967) and *The Apprentice* (1970) both proceed from sexual corruption to general moral degradation and crime. His films since then, including two for the NFB, have usually involved others' scripts and lack the personal touch of the first six. Kent's early work was marked by experimentation and stylization—nervy camera movements, flashback and fantasy sequences, dialogue improvisation, and, in *High*, variation of colour, tinted, and monochrome stock .

Morrie Ruvinsky's *The Plastic Mile* (1968), about a film-director making his first feature, ran afoul of the B.C. Censors for its sex scenes; a screening at the Vancouver Film Festival was cancelled. The film, which incorporated experimental fantasy-sequences and flashbacks, fared better in Europe and was bought by an American company, re-cut with extensive new footage, and retitled *The Finishing Touch* (released 1972). Inspired by the example of Kent and Ruvinsky (who both found funds at U.B.C.), **Jack Darcus** made *Great Coups of History* (1969). An accomplished painter, Darcus learnt his skills on the job from his cameraman Terry Hudson, who had worked with Ruvinsky. Less concerned with breaking taboos than other campus underground films, *Great Coups* nevertheless showed a taste for experimentation by layering narrative: scenes of an interview with an ageing woman reminiscing about living off the men she has picked up are intercut with the dramatization of one such affair and scenes showing the effect of her lifestyle on her maturing daughter. With *Proxy Hawks* (1972) and *Wolfpen Principle* (1973) Darcus used a relationship that develops between a man and beasts in captivity to symbolize the human condition in terms that reminded John Hofsess of D.H. Lawrence: in *Proxy Hawks* a captive hawk comes between an artist and the woman he lives with and gradually undermines the woman's image of her companion; in *Wolfpen Principle* a man becomes obsessed with restoring the wolves he visits nightly at the zoo to their natural state. Looking back to the Vietnam war in *Deserters* (1983), Darcus dramatized an American draft-resister's arrival—with an officer ostensibly on his trail—at the home of a sympathetic Canadian border-crossing guard. It took ten years for Darcus to turn his script for

Overnight (1985) into a film; this comedy with Gale Garnett and Alan Scarfe, set in the world of pornographic film-making, now seems to be circulating on Pay-TV under the title *Not Just A Dirty, Little Movie*.

On the fringes of McGill University, **Frank Vitale**, with Allan Moyle, made *Montreal Main* (1974), an improvised drama that the actors developed by playing themselves; it concerns a latent homosexual relationship between a hippie-artist (played by Vitale) on the Main (Bd. St-Laurent) and an adolescent boy from a slightly bohemian suburban family (Johnny, Dave, and Ann Sutherland)—set along the geographic and socio-cultural boundaries in Montreal that divide the bourgeoisie from the marginal underclasses, the 'straights' from the 'gays', the anglophones from the francophones, and so on. In a similar vein, *The Rubber Gun* (Allan Moyle, 1977), with Vitale on camera, was begun shortly after *Montreal Main* and featured Allan Moyle as a McGill sociology student and Stephen Lack as an artist. Its semi-autobiographical portrayal of life in the drug-counter-culture, its improvisational acting style, and its intricate group relationships recall such French-language films as Jutra's *A tout prendre* and the films of Le Grand Cirque Ordinaire.

REGIONAL FILM

A film shot on location with a strong sense of local colour does not constitute regional film-making. Such works can derive a regional colouring from their scripts, *The Rowdyman* (1971), for example, semi-autobiographically written by Newfoundlander Gordon Pinsent; *Paperback Hero* (1973), written by the Saskatchewan-born Barry Pearson with Les Rose; and adaptations of prairie novels such as Max Braithwaite's *Why Shoot the Teacher* and W.O. Mitchell's *Who Has Seen the Wind*. But true regional film-making is represented by the work of local companies and directors committed to making films that dwell upon a particular region's pictorial qualities, social problems, and dilemmas.

With *John and the Missus* (1985) **Gordon Pinsent** made his own Newfoundland film, adapting it from his own novel, directing it, and playing (**CFA**) John Munn, a hold-out in a Newfoundland outport in 1963 when the copper mine is closed and the government moves to resettle the local inhabitants. Lovingly shot by Frank Tidy, produced by Peter O'Brian (of *The Grey Fox* and *My American Cousin*), and played by a strong cast that included Jackie Burroughs as 'the Missus', the film is a stunning testimony to Pinsent's attachment to his roots, although to some viewers the picture of the outport community seemed too glossy and the nostalgia too rosy. Critics such as John Harkness found *The Adventure of Faustus Bidgood* (**Michael and Andy Jones**, 1986) refreshing. Despite the technical shortcomings of this independent production (ten years in the making), its parallel day-in-the-life stories of a clerk in the Department of Education and of the same man as President of Newfoundland offer a wild, zany satire of the life and dreams of Newfoundlanders.

In Nova Scotia, **Daniel Petrie**'s return from Hollywood to direct his screenplay of *The Bay Boy* (6 **CFA**s, 1983)—a semi-autobiographical coming-of-age story, set in the Glace Bay of the 1930s—can be compared with Pinsent's homages to Newfoundland. More influential than such occasional works has been the role of the Atlantic Filmmakers' Co-op, with the assistance of the regional offices of the NFB and the CBC. The feature film company of Picture Plant arose from it in 1979, with Newfoundlander **Bill MacGillivray** directing, Gordon Parsons producing, and Lionel Simmons on camera. They have deliberately chosen to remain 'outside the slipstream of competition' of major film-making centres, more to avoid artistic compromise than because of regional loyalties. The short feature *Aerial View* (1979), and the features *Stations* (1984) and *Life Classes* (awaiting release), are stories about characters who suffer loss of family ties or friendship and find personal and social identity in cultural expression (as architect, TV journalist—both played by Newfoundland director Mike Jones—or painter) before returning to their roots. The first two films switch back and forth between unstaged home-movie footage (of the actor's own youth, in one case) and scripted dramatic action, and then back to standard documentary with voice-over; they counterpoint sound and image, and unsettle the sense of traditional narrative time by manipulating past and present in a way that underlines the sense of loss.

Surfacing Films (now Salter Street Films), founded by the Donovan brothers (**Paul Donovan** directing, Michael producing), took advantage of tax shelter financing for features. After the failure of *South Pacific - '42* (1980)—a black comedy set on a Canadian submarine in the Second World War—they aimed for the exploitation market with *Siege* (1982), in which a gang of homophobic rednecks lays violent siege to a group of young people during a Halifax police strike, and *Def-Con 4* (1984), a science-fiction action film set in the aftermath of a nuclear holocaust. In the regions, low-budget commercialism is the alternative to low-budget art film.

The focal point for film-making in Manitoba came in 1974 with the arrival of the NFB's regional film office and the establishment of the Winnipeg Film Group (WFG), a co-operative of about thirty members. The first fictional feature from WFG was *The Mourning Suit* (1975) by **Leonard Yakir** who, like many other regional film-makers, used autobiographical detail. Set in Winnipeg's North End, it portrayed a young cellist (Allan Moyle) caught in a crisis of personal relationships with his Jewish mother and his ex-girl-friend, who develops a relationship with his neighbour, the elderly Jewish tailor who makes him a mourning suit. The most prominent film-maker to emerge from the WFG has been **Arthur Kroeker**, who adapted several short stories to film before directing a big-budget feature for TV. Four of Kroeker's award-winning shorts were adaptations of stories by W.D. Valgardson, set in the Icelandic communities around Gimli, Man. The best of these, his short feature *The Pedlar* (NFB, 1982), concerns a tattoo-covered pedlar-cum-juggler on the roads of Manitoba's Interlake area who comes upon a family anxious to marry off their pregnant daughter. *Heaven on Earth* (1986), a feature shot in Ontario from a script by Margaret Atwood and Peter Pearson, depicted the experiences of a number of 'home children' (orphans shipped over from Britain to good Christian families) before the First World War.

The Alberta film industry developed its own infrastructure to assert independence from central Canada: co-operative film-making (Filmwest Associates from 1971), an annual awards ceremony (instituted in 1974), the NFB's Northwest Studio (from 1978), and an Alberta Motion Picture Development Corporation (from 1982)—not to mention producer Fil Fraser's efforts to launch an industry with Narizzano's *Why Shoot the Teacher* in 1977, and as a founder of Albertan film festivals, such as Banff's international TV film festival in 1979. The most successful work has come from writer Sharon Riis and director Anne Wheeler. Riis's story for Fraser's production of *Latitude 55* (John Juliani, 1983) recalls the French short film classic *Incident at Owl Creek* (Robert Enrico, 1961) with its tale of a woman (Andrée Pelletier) caught with a stalled car in a prairie snowstorm and her ensuing relationship with an enigmatic potato farmer (August Schellenberg). After completing some important documentaries **Anne Wheeler** moved into drama and, with Riis's scripts, made the short feature *Change of Heart* (1983), an NFB/CBC co-production in the 'For the Record' series, and the feature *Loyalties* (1985), both of which show the events leading up to the moment of truth when a woman decides she must leave her husband. Set in Lac La Biche, *Loyalties* builds its drama from the parallel marriages of the Suttons, middle-class British immigrants (Susan Wooldridge and Kenneth Walsh), and the poor Métis Rosanne and Eddy (Tantoo Cardinal and Tom Jackson), whose lives intersect when Rosanne is hired to help Lily Sutton settle in.

Vancouver-based **Zale Dalen**'s features were set in British Columbia and the Prairies respectively: *Skip Tracer* (1976) and *The Hounds of Notre Dame* (1980) are low-key dramas based on potentially unsympathetic male protagonists: a collection agent for a Vancouver loan company (David Petersen), and Father Athol Murray (Thomas Peacocke, **CFA**), the renegade founder of Notre Dame College in Wilcox, Sask., famous for its tough methods and ice-hockey. Both films show moments of personal crisis and expose the human qualities masked by their protagonists' unappealing personae.

Phillip Borsos, originally from Tasmania, studied in art schools in both Banff and Vancouver before going into business with commercials, sponsored films, and award-winning documentaries. He made one of the most widely-admired Canadian films, *The Grey Fox* (1980), the story of Bill Miner (Richard Farnsworth), an elderly American stagecoach robber. After a lengthy jail term, Miner robs a train and flees to a mining town in British Columbia, where he almost settles down with a radical feminist (Jackie Burroughs)—before robbing one more train. A quiet alternative to the Hollywood Western, *The Grey Fox* included scenes from a primitive silent Western (Porter's *The Great Train Robbery*, 1903) in a movie-house scene that inspires Miner to switch to train robbery—a device that recalls Borsos' use of early archival footage in his craft documentaries. Borsos abandoned the regional thrust of his early work to make *One Magic Christmas*

(1985), a charming family story set in southern Ontario (partially substituting for an American location) that recalls Frank Capra's *It's a Wonderful Life*.

Charles Wilkinson's *My Kind of Town* (1985) was improvised on an NFB documentary about the full-wall paintings that decorate houses in the declining mill-town of Chemainus, B.C. to create a low-key teenage romantic drama. **Sandy Wilson**'s *My American Cousin* (1985), showered with awards, is one of the best of the regional autobiographical dramas. Set in the Okanagan valley, it portrays in a good-humoured and relaxed style the events of a thirteen-year-old girl's summer in her family home overlooking the lake. Richard Leiterman's photography and Phil Schmidt's art direction recapture the garish colours and trappings of fifties fashions and the awe in which everything American was held—all brought together in the American cousin and his red Cadillac convertible.

HOLLYWOOD NORTH, TV DEALS, AND THE EIGHTIES

Branch-plant film-making became the norm in English-Canadian production with the Capital Cost Allowance program and the advantageous dollar exchange in the seventies and eighties. The director that best typifies the field is **Bob Clark**, whose films draw on bankable genres and plots: *Black Christmas* (1974), starring Andrea Martin and Margot Kidder in nights of terror at the sorority house; *Murder by Decree* (1978), a Canada/UK co-production in which Sherlock Holmes (Christopher Plummer) confronts Jack the Ripper; and *Porky's* (1981; and its first sequel *Porky's II*, 1982), a raunchy tale of oversexed teenage boys in an encounter with a Florida brothel of the 1950s that overtook Reitman's film *Meatballs* as the record box-office Canadian film; and *A Christmas Story* (1983), a broad seasonal comedy set in the forties and based on Jean Sheperd's novel *In God We Trust, All Others Pay Cash*.

The attraction of the commercial genre film is strong for directors resting between TV assignments and more prestigious literary adaptations. After *Wedding in White* **William Fruet** was drawn into violent melodramas for the commercial theatre—*Death Weekend* (1976), *Search and Destroy* (1979), *Cries in the Night* (1980), and *Death Bite* (1982)—in between directing TV dramas such as the award-winning

One of Our Own ('For the Record', 1979), about a boy with Down's syndrome.

This is not to say that the films of Hollywood North are necessarily designed only for teenage drive-ins or late-night pay-TV. Nor are they scorned by the Academy of Canadian Cinema and Television. **Darryl Duke**, a prominent West-coast director in Hollywood (*I Heard the Owl Call My Name* ,1973; and *The Thorn Birds* ,1982–83) and the joint owner of Vancouver's CKVU, directed the Garth Drabinsky production of *The Silent Partner* (1977), a Toronto bank heist movie starring Elliot Gould and Christopher Plummer that collected many **CFA**s, including Best Feature. Drabinsky's production of*The Changeling* (Peter Medak, 1979), a ghost-story starring George C. Scott and Trish Van Devere, won eight **CFA**s, also including Best Feature.

Telefilm's Broadcast Fund not only provided encouragement for mulitple versioned blockbusters like *Joshua Then and Now* and *Les Plouffe*, it also boosted production of short film dramas. Foremost among the producers of these has been the Toronto firm of Atlantis Films. During the eighties they have produced documentaries and adaptations from Canadian short stories by Margaret Lawrence, Alice Munro, Sinclair Ross, W.P. Kinsella, Morley Callaghan, Mordecai Richler, and Hugh Garner. With *Boys and Girls* (**Don McBrearty**, 1984) they won an Oscar, and *The Painted Door* (**Bruce Pittman**, 1985) was nominated for another. Recently they completed two trilogies of stories by Ray Bradbury for Pay-TV. Other longer literary adaptations of the eighties have come from stage director **Robin Phillips'** film of Timothy Findley's *The Wars* (1983), superbly acted by many of Canada's best stage and screen actors. But despite some brilliant moments, it was a two-hour epic made from a three-hour script, and certain crucial episodes and transitions were omitted, including the homosexual scenes that play such an important part in the novel. **Leon Marr**'s *Dancing in the Dark* (1986), from Joan Barfoot's novel, featured a virtuoso performance by Martha Henry as the mad woman reliving her compulsive housewife's existence until the illusion of its stability is shattered in one climactic moment.

Other first features in the eighties came from **Lois Siegel**, who made a series of absurdist sketches into *A Twentieth Century Chocolate Cake* (1983). With *Next of Kin* (1984), **Atom Egoyan** has already drawn critical acclaim for his light-hearted story of a 23-year-old man who lives with his quarrelsome upper-class WASP parents and decides to relinquish this identity and impersonate the long-lost son of a family of Armenian immigrants. After working on the NFB's children's program as well as on his own documentaries, **Michael Rubbo** made one of Pierre Demers series of children's dramas, *The Peanut Butter Solution* (1985), an entertaining story of a boy's trouble with hair—he loses it after a fright and then overtreats it until it grows uncontrollably—that is also about overcoming childhood ghost-fantasies and traumas. **Patricia Rozema**, who had worked with Owen and Cronenberg, made one award-winning short (*Passion: A Letter in 16 mm*) and then went on to success at Cannes with her first feature, *I've Heard The Mermaids Singing* (1987).

6

ANIMATED FILM AND EXPERIMENTAL FILM

ANIMATED FILM

Over the years Academy Awards and Festival Prizes have fuelled Canada's international reputation as a producer of fine animated films, and no survey of film in Canada could be complete without reference to this tradition. Animated film-making is an industry apart—time-consuming and demanding a high degree of graphic imagination and control. In Canada it has flourished both under state production, where animators can achieve a degree of security, and in a private sector dominated by sponsored films and TV commercials, where there may be a steady flow of work but little room to choose subjects. The field of children's cartoons was dominated by the American studios until, through alternative children's TV (such as PBS and CTW), new opportunities emerged for Canadian animators.

Early Canadian animators went south. Montreal caricaturist and painter **Raoul Barré** (1874–1931) pioneered animation techniques in his Bronx studio between 1914 and 1919. Canadian **Stephen Bosustow** founded UPA, a group of disaffected animators who left Disney after the 1941 strike. The first to launch an animation company in Canada (Toronto) was **Bryant Fryer**, a commercial artist from Galt, Ont. From 1927 to 1935 he made six silhouette films that are now in the National Film Archives. Like many of his live-action colleagues, Fryer could not sustain a successful film career. It was the NFB that put Canadian animation on the map.

In 1941 John Grierson brought into the NFB a young Scots graphic artist he had hired in 1936 to make promotional cartoons for the British post office. His job was to round out the Board's wartime programming

112

with publicity spots and sing-along films, and then to establish and train an animation department. **Norman McLaren** (1914–87) became one of the finest animators in the world. He made almost fifty films for the NFB, and won over a hundred international awards. He trained and inspired generations of animators in Canada and elsewhere. Moreover, his work was quite distinct from the school of Disney, Hanna-Barbera, and others.

McLaren began making promotional films for war bonds with *V for Victory* (1941), a series of bouncy animated transformations of the letter V accompanied by a Sousa march. In the sing-along series 'Chants Populaires' McLaren's *C'est l'aviron* (1944) used staggered overlapping mixes to produce the illusion of a canoe's forward movement through landscape hauntingly painted in white gouache. In *La poulette grise* (1947) and *A Phantasy* (1948–52) he experimented with the pastel method, a series of colour transformations of pastel chalk drawings in continuous dissolves. He expanded cameraless animation, painting directly on to the film abstract figures that move rhythmically to music in *Begone Dull Care* (1949); engraving lines on to the film and printing the negative through colour filters on an optical printer in *Lines Vertical* (1962), *Lines Horizontal* (1962), and *Mosaic* (1965). Animated cut-outs appeared in *Rythmetic* (1956) and *Le Merle* (1958). Pixillation (frame-by-frame photography to animate objects or motionless human subjects) was featured in the Oscar-winning *Neighbours* (1952) and in *Opening Speech* (1960). His ballet films *Pas de deux* (1965) and *Narcissus* (1983) used slow motion and chronophotography to achieve a series of superimposed images of filmed dancers in which the parabolic movements and figures are carved in space and frozen in successive poses. McLaren's films go beyond abstract design to reveal process, making us aware of the progressive interventions of the artist, or the logical sequence of a musical form (*Canon*, 1964) or balletic figure (*Pas de deux*). Some project deeply held humanistic beliefs, such as the anti-war parable *Neighbours* or the allegorical revolt of a chair in *The Chairy Tale* (1957). Hand-drawn optical soundtracks produced rhythmic percussive effects in *Dots* (1949), *Loops* (1952), and *Neighbours*, and more elaborate optical forms of synthetic music came from index-cards marked with specific sound-wave patterns. These cards provided visual patterns for a new kind of synaesthesia in *Synchromy* (1971). The performed musical accompaniments range from Oscar Peterson's jazz piano (*Begone Dull Care*) to Ravi Shankar's sitar (*A Chairy Tale*), from Glenn Gould's Bach (*Spheres*) to Romanian panpipes (*Pas de deux*), and include those of the NFB's own Maurice Blackburn and Eldon Rathburn.

In McLaren's films abstraction does not mean they are non-referential. His visual patterns and effects frequently restate a rhythm or pattern already enunciated in a pro-filmic event. When the musical tone and colouring change from one musical segment to another, as in *Begone Dull Care*, the colours and configurations of the patterns and lines change too. Tempo change in the music leads to change in the pacing of the visual movements. When, in *Pas de deux*, the rhythmical movements of the dance are broken into many lines, the lines represent fragmented frozen images of what is performed and normally perceived as continuous movement. Aural and visual rhythms, spatial and temporal patterns are presented simultaneously. They re-present a given pattern by using a different frame of reference, fragmenting it in ways that reveal structure while enhancing its magic. This is the artistic genius of McLaren at work.

By war's end McLaren had assembled a group of gifted animators at the NFB. Many English-Canadians who joined in the first decade came from the Ontario College of Art: Evelyn Lambart, George Dunning, Grant Munro, Robert Verrall, Sidney Goldsmith. **Evelyn Lambart** worked on animating graphics for *Maps in Action* (*WIA*, 1945) and *The Impossible Map* (1947). Others in this generation later made a reputation in the private sector: **George Dunning**, who animated flat metal puppets for the folk song *Cadet Rousselle* (with Low,1947), embarked on a commercial career in Toronto and London that peaked when he headed an international team on the Beatles cartoon *Yellow Submarine* (1968); **Grant Munro**, who helped on several NFB award-winners, worked for Crawley and Dunning's London studio, before turning to documentary; **Jim McKay** introduced the NFB to the now standard cel animation (using layers of celluloid) and other innovations before forming a Toronto company with Dunning (Graphic Associates, now Film Design). **Colin Low**, **Wolf Koenig** and **Robert Verrall** joined at war's end and together made the multi-award-winning *The Romance of Transportation in Canada* (1952), a whimsical pocket history in a simple stripped-down UPA style. Their contemporary **Sidney Goldsmith** acquired an international reputation for animating scientific subjects in *Riches of the Earth* (1954, for the Geological Survey), *Fields of Space* (1969), *Satellites of the Sun* (1974), and *Starlife* (1983), but above all for Kroitor & Low's *Universe* (1960). Beyond Canada he is known for his animation in Stanley Kubrick's *2001: A Space Odyssey* (1968).

In the next two decades the NFB attracted animators from Britain, the U.S., and elsewhere. Before creating his own firm in Montreal, **Gerald Potterton**, who had worked on the British animated feature *Animal Farm* (1954), spent fourteen years at the NFB and is best remembered for two cartoons of stories by Stephen Leacock—the Oscar nominee *My Financial Career* (1962) and *The Awful Fate of Melpomenus Jones* (1983). Potterton's live-action films included *The Railrodder* (1965), a reprise of the old CPR scenics with Buster Keaton crossing Canada on a railway track speeder. In the private sector he made the live-action feature *The Rainbow Boys* (1973) and later directed an international team of animators using full animation and multi-plane camerawork for the full-length Ivan Reitman production *Heavy Metal* (1982). **Derek Lamb**'s NFB work includes two award-winners: *I Know an Old Lady Who Swallowed a Fly* (1964), illustrating the well-known song by Alan Mills, and the didactic *Why Me?* (1978, with Janet Perlman), about one man's struggle to confront the news of impending death. **Michael Mills** came from Britain in 1966 and made the multiple prize-winner *Evolution* (1971), a humorous rendering of the Darwinian thesis. With his own company he won an Oscar nomination for *The History of the World in Three Minutes Flat* (1981). The American humorist and master story-boarder **Don Arioli** wrote ministry-sponsored films, such as the Oscar nominee *The House That Jack Built* (Ron Tunis, 1967), and won **CFA**s for *A Propaganda Message* (Barrie Nelson, 1971) and the hilarious *Hot Stuff* (Zlatko Grgic, 1971). From Denmark came **Kaj Pindal**, best-known for his witty films campaigning against smoking (*King Size*, 1968) and satirizing automania (Oscar nominee *What on Earth !* with Les Drew, 1966). From India, **Ishu Patel** has won recognition for his innovative use of materials and processes: myriads of beads in *Bead Game* (1977); backlit plasticine in *Afterlife* (1978) and *Top Priority* (1981); the experimental Oxberry Animation Camera in *Perspectrum* (1975), for a virtuoso set of variations on eight coloured squares that follow the forms and rhythms of Japanese koto music; and, above all, a volley of animation techniques in the sumptuous *Paradise* (1984), a parable of the blackbird's envy of the bird of paradise. Montrealer **Ryan Larkin** joined in 1964 and animated charcoal drawings to create variations on a theme in continuous transformation, best represented in *Syrinx* (1965).

In 1971 Studio A (for animation) was formed under Wolf Koenig. A new generation arrived, bringing a more personal, even quirky touch. **John Weldon** added an autobiographical flavour to his witty films. *No Apple for Johnny* (1977), which drew on Weldon's own experiences in teacher-training, is described as a 'documentary cartoon'. He also collaborated with **Eunice Macaulay** on the Oscar-winning *Special delivery* (1978), in which the animated action unfolds almost by free association from one man's failure to clear the snow from his walk. **Janet Perlman**'s curious draughtsmanship in *Lady Fishbourne's Complete Guide to Better Table Manners* (1976) echoed the grotesque style of the Polish school, and her Oscar nominee *The Tender Tale of Cinderella Penguin* (1981) adopted medieval pastiche. **Caroline Leaf** animated drawings made of sand on a glass slide lit from below:*The Owl Who Married a Goose* (1974), an Inuit legend with an Inuit soundtrack, *The Street* (1976), from Mordecai Richler's poignant story of Jewish Montreal, and *The Metamorphosis of Mr. Samsa* (1977), from the famous Kafka story. Leaf has since combined animation and live-action film in *Kate and Anna McGarrigle* (1981), about the folk-singing sisters. With experimentalist **Veronika Soul** she made the introspective *Interview* (1979), in which each film-maker embarked on an exploration of the other. **Joyce Borenstein** also used live action, most notably in *The Plant* (with Thomas Vamos, 1983), about a man who takes a plant from the snow into his home with startling results.

In the NFB's Atlantic Region. **Robert Awad** collaborated on a number of satirical pseudo-documentaries combining live-action and animation: *L'affaire Bronswik* (with André Leduc, 1976), *Truck* (1976), and *The National Scream* (with David Verrall, 1980). From the Prairie Region, **Richard Condie** gained international recognition with *The Big Snit* (1985), a macabre film about a grotesque suburban couple who quarrel and make up, oblivious to the outbreak of a nuclear war. In the Pacific Region **Hugh Foulds** is best known for his award-winning *Citizen Harold* (1971), which carried the message of participatory democracy for the Challenge for Change program.

On the French-language side, McLaren recruited graduates from Montreal's École des Beaux-Arts, beginning with **Jean-Paul Ladouceur** and **René Jodoin**, who worked with him on his sing-along films, animating drawings, cutouts, and puppets. Ladouceur's *Chantons Noël* won the first **CFA** for an animated subject in 1949. In the fifties Jodoin began using animation in instructional science films, best seen in *An Introduction to Jet Engines* (1959). In *Ronde Carrée* (1961) and *Notes on a Triangle* (1966) he choreographed geometric shapes to music for mathematics classes. In 1966 Jodoin established a French animation unit and drew together francophone animators scattered throughout the NFB, including Bernard Longpré, Laurent Coderre, and Pierre Hébert.

Bernard Longpré had already completed *Test 0558* (1965), an experiment in mathematical animation. His work under Jodoin recalls experiments of French primitives before 1914: transformations of single-line drawings (*à la* Emile Cohl) in *Nébule* (1973), the fragmentation of the dancing clown-fiddler Paul Cormier and his costume props (*à la* Méliès) in *Monsieur Pointu* (Oscar, 1975), and in a burst of naturalism reminiscent of Ferdinand Zecca, his *One Way Street* (1980) animated line-drawings to show the corrosive effects of alcoholism. **Laurent Coderre** made *Metamorphoses* (1968), animating a juggler who ends up juggling parts of himself, and the extraordinary *Zikkaron* (1971), in which thousands of lino pieces are animated in a series of allegorical transformations. The artist most deeply influenced by McLaren was **Pierre Hébert**, who pioneered new techniques with *Op Hop—Hop Op* (1966), a hand-made scratched-on film using mathematically calculated permutations of 24 basic images, and *Autour de la perception* (1968), with sound-track written on to the film and computer-generated animation of geometric forms and colours. In a second phase Hébert turned to social criticism, using paper cut-out animation in *Père Noël, Père Noël* (1974) to satirize the commercialism of Christmas; *Entre chiens et loup* (1978) used a text by Kurt Weil for a fable on unemployment; *Souvenirs de la guerre* (1982) was an anti-war film. In a third phase Hébert has returned to formal experimentation, particularly in sound-image combinations that retain the strong social conscience: *Etienne et Sara* (1984) shows images of the contemporary world as they appear to a newborn child, and *Chants* *et danse du monde inanimé—le métro* (1984) is a compelling, night-marish vision of the alienating environment of the subway, whose eerie soundtrack by Robert Lepage and René Lussier was recorded at a live showing of the film.

In keeping with the McLaren tradition, artists came from around the world: the Czech **Bretislav Pojar** worked with **Francine Desbiens** on *Balablok* (1972), depicting a war between spheres and cubes, and *'E'* (1981), which animated cut-outs in a fable of totalitarianism. **Lotte Reiniger** made *Aucassin et Nicolette* (1975), a medieval tale brought to life with the delicate silhouettes that made her famous over a fifty-year career in Germany and England. **Alexandre Alexeïeff**, a Russian émigré in France, made *En Passant* (1943), a wartime sing-along film, using his remarkable pin-table: thousands of nails that could be raised or lowered to make pictures when side-lit were used for single-frame animation. Later in the 1960s he donated a miniature pinscreen (10,000 nails) that composer Maurice Blackburn used for his first film *Ciné-crime* (1968). Then in 1972 Alexeieff and his wife Claire Parker returned in person with a full-sized screen (240,000 nails) and from it McLaren directed the demonstrational *Pinscreen* (1973). This so captivated Jacques Drouin that he made *Trois exercices sur l'écran d'épingles d'Alexeïeff* (1974) and then a pocket masterpiece, *Le Paysagiste* (Jacques Drouin, 1976), in which an artist enters his own painted landscape and explores its marvels.

One special initiative of Jodoin's was the development of computer-assisted animation. The seeds for this at the NFB had been sown by Longpré and Hébert. At first such work required the construction of complex algorhythms and animation artists needed the constant assis-tance of a programmer. With interactive picture-driven techniques, using graphic tablets and such, the artist is free to compose the images directly and can use software to supply the intervening stages between images and create the illusion of continuous movement. **Peter Foldès** came from France: his *Metadata* (1971) used a computer without graphic tablet to fill in gaps in a series of line drawings, for example, a landscape that changes from bucolic countryside to urban develop-ment to garbage dump. In the Oscar-winning *La Faim* (1973) more complex line drawings were used and body movement was success-fully synthesized in an allegory of a fat man stuffing himself at the expense of third-world children.

Co Hoedeman's animation of three-dimensional objects featured a twisted wire juggler in *Oddball/Maboule* (1969); Inuit sealskin puppets in *The Owl and the Lemming* (1971) and *The Owl and the Raven* (1973); and foam-rubber puppets in *Le trésor des Grotocéens* (1980). In his Oscar-winning *Le château de sable* (1977) Hoedeman worked with sculpted sand figures. **Suzanne Gervais** has three remarkable works to her credit: *Cycle* (1971), *Climats* (1974), and *La Plage* (1978). **Clorinda Warny** will be remembered for *L'oeuf* (1971), which played obsessively with its central image of an egg, the sardonic *Petit bonheur* (1972), an animated cut-out fable of a mother and child, and *Premiers jours* (completed posthumously by Gervais and Linda Gagnon in 1980), a magical series of metamorphoses, celebrating the integration of nature and humanity.

Outside the NFB film animation has been dominated by companies making TV commercials or freelancing for children's shows like *Sesame Street*: Boxcar, Disada, and Kohill in Montreal, the now defunct Guest Group and Al Guest's newer Rainbow Films, Certified Canadian Content, Cinera, Film Design, and MS Art Services in Toronto, Credo Group and the erstwhile Phillips-Gutkin-Associates in Winnipeg.

The first animated feature film in Canada, *Le Village Enchanté*, was made over six years in the 1950s by a team of animators under **Marcel** and **Réal Racicot**. A pioneering fairy tale, it fits the ideological framework of the first wave of Quebec features and is considered a Disney by-product despite technical flaws. Shot in 16mm., it presumably reached young audiences on alternative circuits since minors were still excluded from Quebec cinemas. Crawley Films in Ottawa produced the second animated feature in Canada, *Return to Oz* (1964), hard on the heels of *The Tales of the Wizard of Oz* (1962), the first Canadian animated TV series.

From 1968 to 1974 Potterton Productions made animated features and short features, including *Tiki-Tiki* (Peter Sanders, 1971), until its live-action work overextended the company and it folded. The animators split into smaller companies: Michael Mills, Disada, and Box Car. Also in Montreal, Les Films Québec-Love used cut-out animation to illustrate popular performances with a nationalist theme by Robert Charlebois and Yvon Deschamps. At Radio-Canada, **Frédéric Back** won an Oscar with his *Crac!* (1982), a coloured-pencil animation of an old rocking-chair that ends up as the most attractive exhibit to visiting children in a museum.

In Toronto the company Nelvana (f.1972) includes **Clive Anthony Smith**, most of whose animated films for young audiences, such as *The Devil and Daniel Mouse* (1978), were made for TV, although recent co-productions—*The Care Bears Movie* (1985) and its sequels—went into theatrical release. From the Winnipeg Film Group (f.1974) came not only Rich Condie but also **Nancy Edell**, whose *Black Pudding* (1969) and *Charley Company* (1972)—extensions of her eccentric drawings—attracted attention at several international Festivals. The Pacific Film Co-op served as a home for many aspiring animators—**Ken Wallace**, for example, whose irreverent *Thanksgiving* (1972) achieved disquietingly surreal effects by animating a trussed turkey. But the West Coast animation scene has been dominated by the prolific **Al Sens** ever since he founded his studio in 1958. To date he has made almost thirty films, usually characterized by his own caustic wit and zany style. He has developed what he calls the 'spit technique . . . drawing and erasing right under the camera . . . (producing) a crude, almost vulgar sort of graphics (that give) vitality to the image and the movement.' His films also incorporate live-action. His work is best represented by *The See Hear Talk Think Dream and Act Film* (1965), a free-flowing run of images whose style has been associated with the Beat culture of Vancouver in the sixties.

EXPERIMENTAL FILM

Experimental film is usually defined as an alternative to other kinds or modes of film: non-commercial (catering to minority tastes and publics), non-industrial (made privately by individuals, often working alone), non-narrative (avoiding plot-lines and identifiable characters), non-representational (abstract or irrational), non-conventional (subversive or even scurrilous). It has been identified with the avant-garde, those artists who radically challenge the norms and forms of the mainstream culture and suggest new aesthetic and philosophical directions. At times film experimentalists have assumed the modernist's task of making evident the materials and processes that constitute the essential nature of film as a distinct medium or the post-modernist's task of making these materials and processes problematic or contradictory. If bibliographic categories like fiction and non-fiction can be used for drama and documentary film, then perhaps poetry is the literary correlate of experimental film. It is difficult to speak of schools since independent experimentalists are often fiercely individualistic. The film-makers themselves are often artists in other media (usually graphic or sculptural) and many of them sustain themselves and their film-making obsession by teaching in colleges and universities.

Demarcation is inevitably arbitrary, since all forms and modes of film can incorporate experimental characteristics—i.e., technical innovations and challenges to formal conventions and norms—often to the chagrin of the experimental purists. In this section, the aim is to introduce some of the film-makers whose work has challenged the modes of construction and reception associated with the entertainment film, the story, and the documentary. Since most readers will only be familiar with experimental film in its more official guises, these films will be discussed briefly before the independent experimentalists of the avant-garde.

Representatives of the official version of the experimental film may be found among the winners of CFAs for best Arts and Experimental Film, a category that existed off and on from 1958 to 1976. During that time fourteen awards were given: nine went to NFB films, three of which were the work of Norman McLaren. Only the final award went to an independent avant-garde experimentalist—**Bruce Elder** for his *Barbara Is a Vision of Loveliness* (1976). The work of NFB innovators, described by Seth Feldman as 'the institutionalized experimental film', was kept for the most part to the safer confines of the animation units and studios. The 1986–87 NFB English and French catalogues taken together list over seventy films as 'Experimental'. Almost three-quarters of these are animated, half of them by McLaren. The best-known NFB experimental film-makers who were not animators are Arthur Lipsett and Derek May.

Arthur Lipsett's fate at the NFB reinforced the avant-garde's belief that experimental film-making at the NFB is an impossible proposition. His collages of found photos and recorded fragments of speech, often out-takes from NFB documentaries, were not always taken seriously there, although he did win an Oscar nomination for his first short, *Very Nice, Very Nice* (1961). In *21-87* (1964), *Free Fall* (1964), *A Trip Down Memory Lane* (1965), and *Fluxes* (1967), his eccentric 'embezzlement of the familiar', as surrealist historians would call it—achieved through decontextualizing fragments of the found world and re-organizing them to fit a black, ironic vision of contemporary life—was seen by many as anarchic. Unfortunately, the NFB soon lost patience with him and his mental health began to deteriorate. In 1970 he left the NFB and made only one or two more films before ending his own life in 1986.

Derek May's films combine experimental and documentary styles and have a personal flavour reminiscent of the Pool-system days. He shows certain preoccupations held in common with less official experimentalists. In *Angel* (1966, **CFA**) May manipulates photographic images with the optical printer by removing all shades of grey to produce a starkly black and white film of a simple male-female encounter, and in *Pandora* (1971) he exploits the disorienting possibilities of selective framing and focusing in a fantasy on the Pandora myth. *Sananguagat: Inuit Masterworks* (1974) and *Pictures from the 1930s* (1977) are concerned with mediations of landscape through art. The feature-length *A Film For Max* (1971) is a diary film of life in the film-maker's family (of three), that led into the cross-cultural tensions and the immigrant's quest for identity explored in *Mother Tongue* (1979)—about the marriage between a unilingual British immigrant (May himself) and a Québécois actress (his wife Patricia Nolin)—and *Other Tongues* (1984), an improvised drama set in Montreal's multicultural St-Louis district.

But experimental film has flowered mainly outside the NFB. In the 1960s the first signs of an interest in avant-garde film came from the campus underground who were reading Jonas Mekas' American journal of avant-garde film *Film Culture* and discovering such film-makers as Kenneth Anger, Stan Brakhage, and Bruce Baillie. From McMaster University, for example, came Peter Rowe and John Hofsess, who both made experimental films there in the sixties (as indicated in Chapter 5), and Bob Fothergill and Bruce Elder who would later play an important role in Toronto. Toronto-based artist **Morley Markson**, whose photographic installation *Kaleidoscope* attracted attention at Expo '67, made several experimental shorts, including a flicker film called *Eyebang* (1968) that was reminiscent of the work of American Paul Sharits, but he also made features that plunged into the visionary obsessions of the contemporary counter-culture. In *The Tragic Diary of Zero the Fool* (1970) three actors, improvising on characters taken from the Tarot pack, struggle against their fate and the forceful control of the director in acts of self-realization; *Breathing Together: Revolution of the Electric Family* (1970), an experimental document loosely centred on the trial of the Chicago Seven, incorporated newsreel, video, and direct interviews to catch the mood of radical change and utopian optimism; *Monkeys in the Attic* (1974), featuring Jackie Burroughs and Louis Del Grande among others, dramatized the clash of culture and counter-culture in one wild fantasy-driven night in a Toronto mansion. In Quebec **Guy Borremans** achieved notoriety in the ciné-clubs with *La Femme-image* (1960), a celebration of erotic desire in which many viewers saw a 1920s surrealist quality, but the film has been denounced by more committed critics as 'reactionary' for its internalization of desire and its objectification of women.

To nurture the growth and public exposure of experimental films, efforts were made to emulate the New York Film-makers Co-operative, founded in 1962 to stimulate independent and experimental film distribution. Toronto's Canadian Filmmakers Distribution Centre (CFMDC), established in 1967 to distribute prints of films by any independent Canadian film-maker on request, has built a major collection of Canadian experimental films and work by leading experimental artists of the United States; Montreal's Co-opérative des cinéastes indépendants (CCI), founded in the same year, has organized local festivals of international independent film and travelling exhibitions of experimental work throughout Canada and Europe, and opened its own Cinéma Parallèle on Montreal's Bd St-Laurent in 1978. By 1979, CFMDC had opened Canadian Filmmakers' Distribution West in Vancouver, and by 1982 it had become an independent entity. In the last two decades local production co-operatives in various Canadian centres have also distributed their own work and acquired collections. Toronto's Filmmakers' Co-op ran from 1971 to 1978 and distributed largely through CFMDC, and as it began to break up, other artist film-makers were developing their own exhibition, distribution, and production centre, The Funnel, founded in 1977. Since 1981 The Funnel has developed its own collection, marked by an emphasis on films in smaller gauges—Super 8, especially; film-performance, or films that integrate a live performance by the artist into a projection of the film; and film as part of mixed-media presentations.

Canada's major experimental film-makers are Michael Snow, Joyce Wieland, Bruce Elder, Al Razutis, David Rimmer, and the late Jack Chambers. All have gained international reputations and played important roles in the establishment of experimental film in Canada. Although their work merits extensive analysis, only the briefest conspectus lies within the scope of this book.

Michael Snow and **Joyce Wieland**, both well-established artists in other media, first made reputations as film-makers while living in New York in the sixties. Their work is exemplary of structural film, an offshoot of the modernist tradition that reduced film to minimal forms—using such devices as sound or film loops (the same fragment repeated) and optical printers that re-process and transform the photographic image—and thereby heightened the awareness of space and time as experienced through film. Of his dozen or so films, the works that built Snow's reputation are those in which a fixed camera engages in one obsessive operation throughout: in *Wavelength* (1967) it is a forty-five-minute forward zoom—jerky and intermittently halted—across an eighty-foot loft towards a still photograph of ocean waves pinned on the wall opposite; in ↔ *Back and Forth* (1969) it is the carefully modulated scanning of a camera from side to side inside a classroom; in *La Région Centrale* the camera is mounted on a computerized carrier programmed to perform movements in circles, parabolas, spirals, and zig-zags across a barren mountain landscape north of Sept-Îles, Quebec. In the first two, human events occasionally intrude into the frame and deflect our attention towards the world represented, but always we are obsessively jerked back into a contemplation of the relentless motion and formal variation that structure the work. The films act as metaphors of consciousness: the move from uncertainty to certainty with the zoom's ever-decreasing field of view, the balancing of opposites back and forth, the sense of the perceiving mind locked in the centre point of a sphere of reality. A more impish side to Snow's film may be seen in the four-and-a-half-hour *Rameau's Nephew by Diderot (Thanx to Dennis Young) by Wilma Schoen* (1974), a twenty-five part series of sketches, sequences, and interludes full of word-play and visual punning that only makes sparse, symbolic allusions to the text of the title. It gave roles to the New York scholars (Jonas Mekas, P. Adams Sitney, and Annette Michaelson) who had championed his earlier work.

Joyce Wieland's work is less complex than Snow's but in some respects shares its impish qualities, which are most evident in her comic fantasy about life in Canada, *Rat Life and Diet in North America* (1968). *Sailboat* (1967), which used repeated shots of a sailboat on a lake seen from shore, accompanied by the sound of crashing waves, has a child-like playful quality, while *1933* (1967) and *Handtinting* (1967) include extensive use of film loops. *La raison avant la passion / Reason Over Passion* (1969) combined views of a journey across Canada with variations on the letters of Prime Minister Trudeau's celebrated dictum in the title; this was recognized as her best work by Sitney, who called it 'a lyric vision tempered by an aggressive and a visionary patriotism mixed with ironic self parody'. It followed *Rat Life* in a trilogy called 'True Patriot Love' that culminated with the theatrical feature *The Far Shore* (1975), a story set in 1919 in Toronto about a woman who is married to a boorish young engineer and becomes attracted to her husband's friend, a northern landscape painter. The film did not do well because many people thought that its vision of the Canadian artistic sensibility was diminished by mannered symbolism and stylized characterization, and Wieland abandoned filmmaking for her work in quilts and wall-hangings. In 1987 her film work was the object of a major retrospective exhibition at the Art Gallery of Ontario, and occasioned the completion of some unfinished projects as well as the release of Kay Armatage's documentary-homage *Artist on Fire*.

Bruce Elder is the third of the major Toronto-based experimentalists. A teacher of film at Ryerson Polytechnic who was trained in philosophy, he has worked tirelessly as an apostle for experimental film in Canada, to encourage not only such film-making but a better awareness of the traditions that have fostered it. Critics tend to make a division between his lyrical pieces, the 'tone poem of waiting and anticipation' *She Is Away* (1975) and the astonishing transformations of dance figures through swirling co-ordinated camera movements, optical printing, and re-sequencing in *Unremitting Tenderness* (1977) and *Look! We Have Come Through!* (1978), and the longer works that began using material from his own film diaries, starting with *The Art* *of Wordly Wisdom* (1979). The longer works culminated in two prodigious films: *Illuminated Texts* (1983), a three-hour work that included a dramatic performance from Ionesco's *The Lesson*, and spoken and written texts over a wealth of images described by Bart Testa as an 'inexorable movement from paradise to apocalypse' and closed with images of the Holocaust; and *Lamentations: A Monument to Lost Civilizations*, an eight-hour marathon that had its première in Elder's 1985 film retrospective at the Art Gallery of Ontario. These two films are to be followed by *Consolations*, currently in progress.

David Rimmer, a Vancouver teacher, has made minimalist films that transform fragments of film into meditations on the nature of film material and our perception of it. *Variations on a Cellophane Wrapper* (1970) and *Seashore* (1971) used film loops in a series of reversals and variations composed on an optical printer. *Surfacing on the Thames* (1970) and *Watching for the Queen* (1973) took anonymous found footage and presented the frames separately in a carefully modulated collage sequence. *Canadian Pacific* (1974) and *Canadian Pacific II* (1975) were composed of shots filmed from a warehouse window overlooking Vancouver Harbour over a period of many months. Connected by dissolves, they show the transformations of the landscape through all weathers and seasons. At times we are aware of the vertical surface of the window (because of rain or a rectangle taped on the pane that makes a second frame), at others we yield to the illusion of three-dimensional space beyond the window, and once or twice we become aware of the space behind the camera in the reflection on the glass.

Jack Chambers was the best known of a group of artists in London, Ont. that also included Keewatin Dewdney and Greg Curnoe. In *Circle* (1968–69) he shot four seconds each day from the same spot in his backyard over a period of one year and edited them together, showing the occasional traces of human life inside the eternal cycle of the natural year. His *Hart of London* (1970) takes news footage of a deer trapped and killed in the city in 1954 and intertwines images from London's past with images of life and death, the most graphic being the juxtaposition of childbirth with a hyperrealistic scene of a dying lamb. Chambers' films demonstrate his interest as a painter in the ambivalent qualities of the photographic image, an interest he expressed in his 1969 manifesto 'Perceptual Realism'. According to

Bruce Elder's penetrating analysis, Chambers demonstrates in *The Hart of London* the constitution of personal identity through the indissoluble linking of self, nature, and community.

Al Razutis is a critic, teacher, and film-maker in Vancouver whose major work is contained in two major cycles: *Amerika* (1972–83), twenty short pieces arranged in three reels, described by Razutis as 'a mosaic that expresses the various sensations, myths, landscapes of the industrialized Western culture'; and *Visual Essays: The Origins of Film* (1973–83), a 'structural investigation of the primitive silent cinema'. In each of these cycles he uses various techniques to transform the image in order to engage in a critique of the established culture and a search for a newer liberating imagery.

Among the many other Canadian experimental film-makers is the expatriate Québécois **Vincent Grenier**. He made films in New York that reflected the minimalist modernism of the early seventies there (*Light Shaft*, 1975 and *X*, 1976), but efforts in his later work to frustrate viewer's expectations through ambiguity and displacement have caused some critics to identify it with post-modern practice (*Plus proche dehors* 1979, *D'après Meg* 1982).The prolific **Rick Hancox** has combined poetic texts with film images in a trilogy—*Waterworx* (1982), *Landfall* (1983), and *Beach Events* (1984)—and has demonstrated an eye for the absurd in *Wild Synch* (1973) and *Zum Ditter* (1979). Films such as **Keith Lock**'s feature *Everything, Everywhere, Again, Alive* (1974) or **Barbara Sternberg**'s *Trilogy* (1985) use various repetitive figures and prosodic devices to turn personal diary footage into meditative reflections on human time, natural cycles, and cosmic mystery. In *The Road Ended at the Beach* (1983) and *?O,Zoo! (The Making of a Fiction Film)* (1986) **Phil Hoffman** has played with the diary form to examine ways in which narrative logic intervenes to structure personal memory and give meaning to past experience. Based in Kingston, **Blaine Allen** pursued a similar examination of the process of fictional construction in *Yukon Postcards* (1983), which combines still snapshots and a spoken account of incidents around a northern mine. The interest in photographic representations of landscape recur in **Andrew Lugg**'s *Postcards* and *Black Forest Trading Post* (1976). The extension of experimental interest to alternative forms of narrative, particularly in its association with certain feminist projects (the so-called New Narrative), is illustrated in the work of Vancouver's **Patricia Gruben** (*Sifted Evidence*, 1982 and *Low Visibility*, 1984), and in a different way in **Kay Armatage**'s *Storytelling* (1983), in which the interlacing of seven storytelling performances reveals constants of story form to which she refuses narrative closure. Brenda Longfellow has also documented feminist experimentation in a number of feature films by Quebec film-makers, such as Paule Baillargeon, Léa Pool, and Mireille Dansereau (see Chapter 4), and in *Le journal inachevé* (1983), a deconstructed diary-film by **Marilu Mallet**. On the West Coast, the influence of David Rimmer can be felt in **Tom Braidwood**'s use of looping in *Backbone* (1972) and in *Limited Engagement* (1976), but these films with images of war and a consumer society are more socially engaged than Rimmer's. **Kirk Tougas**'s films, such as *The Politics of Perception* (1973), engage in the progressive reduction of photographic images to their photochemical elements. **Chris Gallagher**'s early short works have culminated in the feature-length *Undivided Attention* (1987), an anthology of perceptual puns, repetitive figures of urban landscapes, and loosely linked scenes of couples.

It is fitting that this book should close with a survey of some of the experimental work being done in Canadian film, for of all film-makers the experimentalists have the greatest difficulty in reaching an audience. Yet these artists often manage to project the most moving, the most challenging, or the most provocative picture of the world we live in. In recent months a debate exploded from the columns of *Canadian Forum*, in which Bruce Elder's manifesto on 'The Cinema We Need ' (see *Canadian Forum*, Vol. XLIV, No. 746, Feb. 1985, and *Cinema Canada*, Nos 120-1, Jul.-Aug. 1985) issued a clarion call for a new kind of film-making, one in which the ego of the artist is surrendered to a new spontaneity, a cinema of perceptions and immediate experiences. He claimed that only the avant-garde gave any sign of undertaking such an enterprise. Those who upheld the view that Canadian film should project a realistic image of the national culture to the greatest number wasted no time in roundly condemning Elder as an elitist and a self-interested idealist. It is my hope that this reaction will not prevail and that in future the audience for experimental film can be expanded so that many more Canadians will come to know and appreciate this rich local tradition.

FOR FURTHER STUDY

FILM ANTHOLOGIES AND FILMS ABOUT CANADIAN FILM

'Self-Portrait' (5 parts, Guy Glover, NFB, 1961)—a series of extracts from NFB films 1939–60

'How They Saw Us' (8 parts, Ann Pearson, NFB, 1977)—a series of NFB films on women, 1942–57

The Image Makers (Albert Kish, NFB, 1980), a montage of extracts celebrating the NFB's fortieth anniversary

The Working Class on Film (NFB, 1975), extracts from fifty years of Griersonian documentary

Hors d'oeuvre (Potterton/Verrall/Lipsett, NFB, 1960), an anthology of NFB animated film

The Light Fantastick (Glover/Patenaude, NFB, 1974), an anthology of NFB animated film

Pot-Pourri (NFB, 1962), an anthology of NFB animated film

Dreamland: A History of Early Canadian Movies, 1895–1939 (Donald Brittain, NFB, 1974), a documentary with extracts from films of the period

Has Anyone Here Seen Canada? A History of Canadian Movies 1939–53 (Kramer, NFB, 1978), a documentary with extracts from films of the period

'Cinéma d'ici' (11 parts, Radio-Canada, 1972), a documentary history of Quebec cinema, with interviews and extracts

Cinéma, cinéma (Gilles Carle/Werner Nold, NFB, 1985), a documentary of 25 years of NFB French films

Backlot Canadiana (Peter Rowe, 1975), a documentary on the Canadian Co-operative Project

FILMS ABOUT CANADIAN FILM-MAKERS

Chambers: Tracks and Gestures (John Walker/Christopher Lowry, 1982)
Grierson (Roger Blais & James Beveridge, NFB, 1973)
Co Hoedeman, Animator (Nico Crama, NFB, 1981)
Eve Lambart (Margaret Wescott, NFB, 1978)

Looking for Martin Lavut (Al Maciulis, 1985)
The Eye Hears, The Ear Sees (BBC, 1970), on Norman McLaren
Window on Canada #29 (NFB, 1954), on Norman McLaren
Les Traces du rêve (Jean-Daniel Lafond, NFB, 1986), on Pierre Perrault
Laugh Lines: A Profile of Kaj Pindal (Zina Heczko/Franco Battista, NFB, 1979)
Snowscreen: The Art of Michael Snow (Robert Shoub, 1984)
A Film About Joyce Wieland (Judy Steed, 1972)
Artist on Fire (Kay Armatage,1987)

BOOKS IN ENGLISH

For a more detailed bibliography see MORRIS. PETER. *The Film Companion*. Toronto, Irwin Publishing, 1984, pages 333-5 and under individual entries. The following is a selection of recent books:

DEAN, MALCOLM. *Censored! Only in Canada*. Toronto, Virgo Press, 1981.

EVANS, GARY. *John Grierson and the National Film Board: The Politics of Wartime Propaganda* . Toronto, University of Toronto Press, 1984.

FELDMAN, SETH, ed. *Take Two*. Toronto, Irwin Publishing, 1984.

FETHERLING, DOUG. *The Blue Notebook: Reports on Canadian Culture*. Oakville, Mosaic Press, 1985.

JAFFE, CHAPELLE, ed. *Who's Who in Canadian Film and Television*. Toronto, Academy of Canadian Cinema & Television, 1986.

JONES, D. B. *Movies and Memoranda. An Interpretative History of the National Film Board of Canada*. Ottawa, C.F.I./Deneau, 1981.

PRATLEY, GERALD. *Torn Sprockets: The Uncertain Projection of the Canadian Film*. New Jersey, Associated Universities Press, 1987.

SCOTT, JAY. *Midnight Matinees*. Toronto, Oxford University Press, 1985.

TOPALOVICH, MARIA. *The Canadian Film Awards*. Toronto, Academy of Canadian Cinema, 1984.

WALZ, GENE, ed. *Flashback: People and Institutions in Canadian Cinema*. Montreal, Médiatexte, 1986.

WEES, WILLIAM C. and MICHAEL DORLAND, eds. *Words & Moving Images*. Montreal, Médiatexte, 1983 (some essays in French).

BOOKS IN FRENCH

For a detailed bibliography see FOURNIER-RENAUD, MADELEINE AND PIERRE VÉRONNEAU. *Écrits sur le cinéma (bibliographie québécoise 1911–1981)*. Montreal, la cinémathèque québécoise, 1982 *Dossiers de la cinémathèque* 9. Annually updated in *Copie Zéro* in 'Annuaire de longs métrages'. A select bibliography of recent work follows.

CARRIÈRE, LOUISE. *Femmes et cinéma québécois*. Montreal, Boréal Express, 1983.

HOULE, MICHEL AND ALAIN JULIEN. *Dictionnaire du cinéma québécois*. Montreal, Fides, 1978.

LAMONDE, YVES & PIERRE-FRANÇOIS HÉBERT (eds.). *Le Cinéma au Québec. Essai de statistique historique (1896 à nos jours)*. Québec, Institut québécois de recherche sur la culture, 1981.

LEBOUTTE, PATRICK, ed. *Cinémas du Québec au fil du direct*. Éditions Yellow Now, Crisnée (Liège), 1986.

LEVER, YVES. *Histoire du cinéma au Québec*. Québec: Ministère de l'éducation, Direction général de l'enseignement collégial, 1983.

MAJOR, GINETTE. *Le cinéma québécois à la recherche d'un public. Bilan d'une décennie: 1970–1980*. Montreal, Presses de l'Université de Montréal, 1982.

PAGEAU, PIERRE & YVES LEVER. *Cinémas canadien et québécois. Notes historiques*. Montreal, Collège Ahuntsic, 1977.

VÉRONNEAU, PIERRE, MICHAEL DORLAND, and SETH FELDMAN. *Dialogue*. Montreal, Médiatexte, 1987 (one-third of the articles in English).

Dossiers de la cinémathèque, Montreal, la cinémathèque québécoise.

  3. VÉRONNEAU, PIERRE, ed. *Le Succes est au film parlant francais (Histoire du cinema au Québec 1)*. 1979.

  5. VÉRONNEAU, PIERRE, ed. *L'Office National du Film l'enfant martyr*. 1979.

  7. VÉRONNEAU, PIERRE, ed. *Cinema de l'époque duplessiste (Histoire du cinema au Québec 11)*. 1979.

  9. *Ecritures de Pierre Perrault*. Actes du colloque 'Gens de paroles' à La Rochelle, France, 1982. Published 1983.

 12. *Le cinéma: théorie et discours*. Actes du colloque de l'Association québécoise des études cinématographiques, 1983. Published 1984.

 14. FAUCHER, CAROL, ed. *La production française à l' ONF. 25 ans en perspective*. 1984.

 15. LACASSE, GERMAIN. *L'Historiographe: Les débuts du spectacle cinématographe au Québec*. 1985.

INDEX

(CHIEFLY OF FILM-MAKERS)